açai strong
transform into
a remarkable company

açai strong
transform into
a remarkable company

Wusu Dumbuya Jr.
Designed by Demetra Baylor

Global Publishing
& Media Group

LONDON   PARIS   NEW YORK
WASHINGTON, DC   SYDNEY

Published by (GPMG) BUSINESS a division of Global Publishing & Media Group

Global Publishing
& Media Group

Global Publishing & Media Group (GPMG)
4753 West Braddock Road, Suite 10,
Alexandria, Virginia 22311 USA

Library of Congress Control Number: 2013945630

ISBN: 978-0-9860426-0-7
ISBN: 978-0-9860426-1-4 (EBook)
ISBN: 0986042609

Designed and Printed in the United States of America
Cover and Interior Designed by Demetra Baylor
(www.demetrabaylor.com)

For Demetra, Zoë, my parents, the Baylors, and the Deans
Thank you for your unwavering support.

Praise For Açai Strong

"Açai Strong shows how emotional labor, openness, and art can come together to change your business."
—*Fast Company*

"This is what the future of business looks like: emotional labor, art, and brands that harness genius into their products. Actually, it's already happening around you."
—*South African Business Report*

"If Wusu Dumbuya didn't exist, we would need to invent him—that's how remarkable he is! You hold in your hands the most compelling, accessible, and purpose-filled business book. Do your business a big favor. Read it. Your future will thank you."
—*Ackmed Sheriff, Founder, Build Africa Project*

"It's easy to see why companies would pay to hear what Dumbuya has to say."
—*South Asia Business Report*

"Thousands of authors write business books every year; only a handful write books that will remain relevant for generations. Fewer still—one, to be exact—can deliver counterintuitive thinking and a great sense of fun. Dumbuya does just that."
—*Entrepreneur Today*

a first look at açai strong

The business world has changed (once again), and the stakes are higher than ever. Today, businesses are facing a full-fledged revolution. We are in an übercompetitive world involving arts, gifts, and the ability for any company to make an indispensable contribution to their products, their consumers, the way they do business, and whatever else they care about. If your company is not indispensable, it's because you have not made the choice to become "Açai Strong." My goal is to help you see that the choice is ultimately yours.

contents

Being able to see

The business models we grew up with are a mess. They are falling apart, and businesses are not scared. These companies are now victims with outdated business models that undervalue them.

A business or company that is remarkable is worth talking about. Worth getting noticed. New, interesting, indispensable, and Açai Strong.

The cause of business failure today is the consumers' desire to turn products and services into replaceable parts in their lives. The easier it is to replace your products and services, the less they have to pay for them.

matters. Then a deadline arrives, and you have to cut it short. Is shipping that important?

chapter 9: açai strong and powerful

In the Pacific Northwest, Native American tribal leaders established power by giving everything away.

chapter 10: gift giving in practice

And so the movement grows.

chapter 11: where is the GPS?

Successful companies are usually able to see the threads of the past and the threads of the future and untangle them into something manageable.

chapter 12: the choice is yours

Will opening longer make you Açai Strong? Does painting more pictures help? Writing more words? Inventing more inventions? To a point, yes…

chapter 13: connecting

The Açai Strong Company will not succeed in isolation.

chapter 14: seven açai strong traits

Is there a list? Yes.

chapter 15: when it doesn't work (well)

Make more ART.

chapter 16: in perspective

All I wanted to do in this book was sell you on being the artist and entrepreneur you really are. What will you choose?

antioxidants

açai strong people and companies

açai strong chews

Food for thought

preface

BEING ABLE TO SEE

The housing bubble busted. It took nearly a decade, but jobs in the industry that were vibrant, profit making, and exciting are nothing but "foreclosed dreams."

The question I would have you wonder about isn't "How could this have happened?" No, the question that's fascinating is "Why did professionals in that industry fail to see it coming?"

Why did homeowners and banks stay on sinking ships when there were warnings and lifeboats nearby?

The bottom line is, if you are not looking, you are not going to see.

If your preference is keeping your eyes closed, don't be surprised if you end up getting surprised.

In the early 2000s, I was hooked into the Internet. I was building a hopeful dating website and running an Internet promotions and marketing company. I was helping friends set up online businesses. Apparently, my eyes were open.

In 2005, I was paid six figures for my dating website.

During that same period of time, for less money, a few guys from Harvard built a company called Facebook.

I'm not an idiot; I merely chose to keep my eyes closed to the social-networking revolution. It cost me millions of dollars and a ride of a lifetime.

A revolution is here again. What's next is important; what's now is more important.

One last thing before we get started: One day, consumers are going to remember what your company did. They may remember that you followed trends or that you were pioneering as a company.

Perhaps, though, we'll remember that you made an impact, a connection, and that you were Açai Strong.

introduction

ARE YOU AN AÇAI STRONG COMPANY?

An Açai Strong company is a company with exceptional abilities and insight to finding the not-so-obvious solutions to a problem. These companies look at something that has average companies stuck and gets to the best solution, while delighting consumers along the way.

Have you ever done that? At least once? No company is Açai Strong all the time. Xerox had trouble finding its way, and in recent years, General Motors reinvented to remain relevant. Like Xerox and GM, all of us can be açai when we need to be. So please don't trade your artistry for momentary stability in following the trend, because the market will change, and you will not be able to reinvent.

Açai Strong is a business manifesto, a plea from me to businesses and the great minds that run them. Right now, I am not focused on the tactics companies use to make products or spread ideas. This is different. This doesn't require you to change the way you run or manage your business, although it challenges the process and energy you put into production.

The business models we grew up with are a mess. They are falling apart, and businesses are not scared. Every day, I see companies that have so much to give, but somehow, they hold it back.

They have become victims with outdated business models that undervalue them.

It's time to stop complying with the system of cheap production methods instead of artistry.

Stop settling for what's tax deductible or can be mass-produced, and start giving gifts and selling products that change people.

For generations, the business world has been seduced, brainwashed, and scammed into fitting in and following trends, research predictions, and statistics. This is no longer the way.

You have brilliance in your company and its products, your contributions are valuable, and the art in your designs are precious. I hope you will stand up and be different. Become Açai Strong.

My intentions are to persuade you to see that there is an opportunity to significantly change the life of your company for the better. Not by doing something easy, but by understanding that the business world has fundamentally changed. By taking advantage of this moment, you will become a company the world believes is indispensable. You, too, can become Açai Strong.

Every day, if you focus on the gifts, arts, and connections that characterize the remarkable companies, you will become a little more indispensable—a little more açai and a little less apple. (Apple Corp. is still açai, by the way.)

1

❖   ❖   ❖

why become açai strong

When my family and I became vegetarians a few years ago, we ate an apple a day. For those years, we marveled at the health benefits we reaped from the apples.

Then, in the past year, we started ignoring apples. Our new craze became açai, a tropical fruit from South America. The apples still had benefits, but what once was amazing was now common. Worse than common, the apples became boring.

Açai, however, was an interesting fruit. It had lots of antioxidants and even tasted better. Frankly, açai is remarkable.

Like açai, this book is about the why, what, and how to make your business remarkable. It is about being fresh and outdoing your competition.

A business that's remarkable is worth talking about, worth getting noticed—exceptional, new, interesting, and indispensable. Its redundancy is invisible. It is Açai Strong.

Remarkable companies use art to build things worth noticing right into their product and service offerings. They do not use last-minute marketing tactics. They understand that if the product itself is not amazing, then it will become invisible.

Today, post-recession consumers are very cautious of the things they buy. They buy only what they need and spend a lot of time researching what they buy.

If your marketing department is taking nearly finished or mediocre products and spending time to communicate its special powers, that approach no longer works.

We have now reached the point where we can no longer make products for the masses. We are living in a world where most companies and their products or services are invisible. Over the past decade, business writers have made the point of a changing business environment. Companies have read, discussed, and even used some of these ideas, but for some reason, they maintain their draconian ways of doing business. Alternative approaches to business are all we have left.

This is why you should put a shot of açai in everything you do. Mass media and social media are no longer secret weapons. What you need are quality products and services. Stop advertising and marketing. Start innovating.

Before the Internet, there was word of mouth. Products and services that could solve problems got talked about and eventually got purchased.

During the Internet era, the combination of social media, increasing prosperity, and the seemingly endless desire for products yielded great successes for companies.

Now that the Internet is settling in, we are back to where we started. But instead of slow word of mouth, there are instant Twitter feeds that will destroy or build the reputation of companies and products in 140 characters or less.

As businesspeople, we know that the old stuff is not working. The reason for this is, as consumers, we no longer want a good commercial to go with average products. We want brilliance in everything a company does. This is why companies like Whole Foods and Samsung are thriving.

In the last decade, we have changed the way we think about business. In fact, most people don't buy your products: either they don't have the money or they don't want them. If your audience is not receptive to your ideas, then you don't have a market.

This was not true all the time, but it is now. We don't have the disposable incomes of before. Today, we find what we really want and buy it at the best possible price. This thinking has allowed Açai Strong companies like Groupon to be successful.

Among the people who will buy from you, a lot of your prospective clients will never hear about you. There are so many alternatives out there that, in order to gain market share, you must be remarkable.

Worse still, people are getting harder to reach. Consumers don't want you to smother them with marketing materials. We need to get better at recognizing what satisfies consumers and even better at delivering it.

Because we have overwhelmed consumers with too much of everything, they are less likely to go out of their way to tell friends and family about your products.

The bottom line is, all the obvious methods no longer work. Consumers are harder to reach. So when you do, cherish their attentions. Satisfied customers don't talk about you like before. The old rules have not worked in the past ten years. Mass marketing is dead, and products with artistry still amaze.

2

❖ ❖ ❖

the old business world
and the opportunity

The first chapter of Adam Smith's *Wealth of Nations* makes it clear that the way for businesses to win is to break up the production of goods into tiny tasks—tasks that can be undertaken by low-paid people following instructions.

For a few hundred years, that was how business worked. What made sense was quantifiable productivity, which, in turn, produced profits.

Our businesses are struggling because, during times of adversity, the very last thing we need is a map to follow. Where are the leaders and innovators of our industries?

That system was simple. Find a large niche not yet over saturated. Build a factory. Buy television advertising. The advertising would lead to sales and bigger distributions, which would keep the factory open and, in turn, create profits.

Astute companies then used the profits to buy more media space. This led to even bigger distribution and sales, and the cycle continued. That's how many brands we know were built. That system worked for Revlon.

That's the problem today. The business paradigm is hemorrhaging. Most businesses and their leaders don't have a clue of what to do about it. Well, the answer is simple: stop creating safe and ordinary products combined with great marketing, and start creating remarkable products that people seek.

Remarkable products should replace average products; then advertise to small niches instead of advertising to anyone, and stop being afraid of failure and make big changes to the culture of your company.

The way to figure out what's working is to look at the world and see what successful companies have in common. Without access to the workings of other companies, that actually may be difficult. I'll give you a little hint. What do Four Seasons and Motel 6 have in common? Or even Walmart and Neiman Marcus, both of which have been growing in the last decade? For starters, they all sell great products.

It can be like trying to drive by only looking in the rearview mirror if your products are lacking. However, what all these companies really have in common is that they don't have anything in common. They are outliers. They are on the fringes. Very exclusive or very cheap. Very big or very small.

The reason it's hard to follow trends is this: The trend is only a trend because it did something indispensable. Something açai. And that remarkable thing has now been done. It's no longer remarkable when you do it.

The businesses of old are quick to defend the power of past successes. They are delighted to point out the great success stories of their past and to happily articulate why their past successes can spearhead their next products or innovations. Look at the brilliant folks at Sony; they, too, are in the dark.

We live in a business world where all the joys and profits have been squeezed out of following the rules. Outsourcing and the new marketing are punishing any company that is merely good and products that are merely designed. Worse still, the type of low-risk, high-stability companies that were once successful are nothing but unfair risks today. You must be agile, adaptable, and açai.

The cause of the suffering is the consumer's desire to turn your business into replaceable parts of their lives. The easier a company's products are to replace, the less they have to pay for them. And, so far, businesses are complicit to this commoditization.

This is your opportunity. The indispensable company brings human touch, connection and art to her consumers. She is the key player, the company whose products and or services are difficult to live without. The company that we build our lives around. You recognize this opportunity to be indispensable, highly sought after and unique. You are Açai Strong. A company worth supporting and keeping.

How is it possible to brainwash hundreds of companies to bury their genius, to give up their visions, and buy into the ideas of following trends?

Part of this was economic, no doubt. But I don't fully believe that this is enough to explain the massive embrace of mediocrity.

In every corporation, in every country in the world, executives are waiting for the next trend. By then, it is too late. So many of us pretend that we would love to have control of our industries. Give our company a chance, and we blow it in a heartbeat.

I have seen this in London, Dubai, Shanghai, Cape Town, and Washington, DC, among many other places. Businesses follow trends because they are scared of figuring it out for themselves.

Every business stands next to other businesses, whether online or offline, each striving to be like the other, but maybe a little better, waiting for the next customer to come along and pick them.

And, of course, the customer picks a particular business. The customer recognizes it or trusts it but, more and more, because it's cheaper. Remember, you are all the same, anyway. Your business has been designed to fit in, and that's the problem. This is uncomfortable, but true.

Consumers are no longer loyal to cheap products. They crave the unique, the remarkable, and the personal—even those trying to save a buck. Sure you can succeed for some time by being the cheapest, but you earn your place in the market with genius.

There are only two choices for businesses today: win by being ordinary and standard, or win by being more remarkable and personal.

OUR WORLD NO LONGER COMPENSATES AVERAGE COMPANIES

There is stress because, for many companies, that's all they know. Business schools and society have reinforced this approach for generations. It turns out that what consumers really need and want are gifts and connections from the products they use and the companies that create them.

Business leaders don't get a map or a set of rules. Leading without a map requires a different attitude. It requires genius. These genius companies are the building blocks of tomorrow's high-value industries.

AÇAI STRONG COMPANIES ARE THE DRIVING FORCE OF OUR FUTURE

The Internet has made it easier to beat your competitors and mediocrity so much harder to sustain.

Gain the right to your consumer's attention. The only way to get what you are worth is to stand out—to be seen as indispensable and to produce the interactions that consumers care about.

3

❖ ❖ ❖

thinking about and understanding your choice

Can you be Açai Strong? Yes. Yes, you can.

This is an important question, and it deserves a thoughtful answer.

The first thing to do is realize that other companies have done this before you. Companies have survived recessions, restructuring, and bankruptcies—and have still done the challenging work to remain in business but, more important, have reinvented themselves with genius.

That's essential to know because that means it's not impossible.

The second thing, even more important than the first, is the companies that have made this transition have nothing on you. Not a single thing.

In every case, the remarkable businesses among us are not the ones created with a magical talent. No, they are companies that have decided that a new kind of work is important, and trained themselves to do it.

BEING REMARKABLE

Where do great restaurants, law firms, technology companies, and hospitals come from?

Explain this: if I make a list of great companies (Target, Walmart, Tumblr, Google, HTC), not one of the names on this particular list is the product of a school designed to create them.

A great business school or business incubator will not keep you from being Açai Strong, but it's usually not sufficient to guarantee you will become so. There is something else at work here.

Harvard Business School might work; lousy schools definitely stack the deck against you. But it seems like schools are working very hard to kill our naturally born artistry.

Let me be clear. Great professors are wonderful. They change lives. We need them. The problem is most schools don't appreciate great professors. These institutions are organized to stamp out excellent thought-provoking professors. Schools bore them, bureaucratize them, and make them curriculum followers.

Today, companies, too, are working hard to bury their genius. Although sometimes hidden, I have never seen a business which had no art. Markets are crying out. We need you to stand up and be remarkable. Be human. Give us less Wi-Fi. Contribute. Interact. Take the risk of making someone upset with your innovation and insight. I promise they will be inspired instead.

Consumers say that all they want is cheap commodities. Given the choice, most of them, most of the time, seek out artistry. We seek out experiences and products that deliver the most value, the most connections—products that change us for the better. You, too, can deliver these things to your consumers.

If you want a company where it's all right to follow trends, don't be surprised if you follow the next trend out of business.

YOUR MARKETPLACE

See your marketplace as being limited, a zero-sum battlefield, and a place where in order for one company to win, another must lose. A place where talent creates growth, in turn increasing market share.

Great vision and talent leads to more innovation and productivity.

As an Açaí Strong company, you can have exceptional productivity, which makes for better efficiency. This solution leads to opportunities for your company and its stakeholders.

The more you win, the more you control your markets.

WILL YOU STILL BE LOVED?

This is the more powerful question, and a difficult one. It is entirely possible that once you chose to become an Açaí Strong company, you will no longer be loved. Not by the same consumers who love you now, perhaps, nor for the same reasons.

But those people will come around, or they never loved you from day one, did they?

THINK ABOUT THIS

It's easy to argue that this genius stuff is for other companies, not you. Those other companies have people with gifts, or genes, or education, or background, or connections. It's easy to fool yourself into believing that genius works for them, but it will not work for you.

But of course. Except, Nelson Mandela changed the world from a jail cell. Except, Steve Jobs was raised by adoptive parents. Except, Cathy Hughes dropped out of the University of Nebraska at Omaha and ended up the first black woman running a publicly traded company in the United States. I don't have room to name the less famous people or companies that had the same, or even less, resources than you but were willing to accept the genius title and make a choice.

THE ENTREPRENEURSHIP DREAM

Do you remember the old "entrepreneurship dream"? It struck a chord with millions of entrepreneurs, in the United States and the rest of the world. Here is how it goes:

1. Write a business plan.
2. Follow your business plan.
3. Have an exit strategy.
4. Work hard.
5. Suck it up if you fail.
...You will be rewarded.

As we've seen, that dream is over. The "new entrepreneurship dream," the one that markets around the world are embracing as fast as they can, is this:

1. Be remarkable.
2. Be generous.
3. Create art.

4. Make judgment calls.

6. Connect people and ideas.

7. Be Açai Strong.

...We have no choice but to reward you.

WHAT WOULD MAKE YOU CONQUER YOUR MARKET?

If your consumers wanted to replace you with a company far better, what would they look for? I think it's unlikely that they would look for a company willing to open later or a company with more industry experience.

No, the competitive advantage the marketplace demands is a company that's more human, connected, and mature. They demand an Açai Strong company with passion and energy, capable of seeing things as they are and negotiating multiple priorities while making insightful decisions without angst. Flexible in the face of change, resilient in the face of confusion and adversity.

All of these attributes are choices, not chapters in your business plan; all of them are available to you.

SECRET MEMO TO COMPANIES

Given the chance, you should choose to be indispensable.

After all, if you are remarkable, the consumer has to treat you better, pay you fairly. You won't be the first to be shown the door in a slow period; in fact, you will be the last.

Not only do you have security, but also you have confidence—the confidence to make a difference in your marketplace and do the work that matters.

If you can be human in your marketplace (not just a company), you will discover a passion for work you did not know you had. When work becomes personal, your customers are more connected and happier. That creates value.

When you are not a profile on Angieslist.com, an easily replaceable commodity, you will get paid what you are worth. Which is much more than you are getting now.

4

❖ ❖ ❖

how did we get here?

"What I want is a company that will do exactly what I tell them to."

"What I want is a company that sells cheap products."

So if this is what the consumer really wants, how come the star companies don't follow these rules? How come the consumers who want the latest released products are wooed to stand in long lines just to be the first to get them?

What the consumers really want is an artist, a company that changes everything, a company that makes dreams come true. What the consumers really want is someone who can see the reality of today and attain a better tomorrow. What the consumers really want is remarkable.

If they can't have that, they'll settle for a cheap company.

MEDIOCRE OBEDIENCE

We've been taught to be average in our markets.

We've been taught to overproduce as a shortcut to success.

We've been taught not to care about our job or our consumers.

And we've been taught to fit in.

None of these attributes helps you get what you deserve or gives your company the value it rightfully deserves.

We've bought into a model that encourages us to embrace the system, advertise for pleasure, and separate ourselves from our work. We've been taught that this approach works, but it doesn't (not anymore). And this disconnect keeps us from succeeding, cripples the growth of our economy, and makes us really stressed (even after retail therapy).

In seems "natural" to live the same life so many of our competitors live, but in fact, it's quite counterproductive. We exist in a corporate-manufacturing mindset, one so complete that any company with genius seems like an oddity. In the last few years, though, it's becoming clear that companies that reject the state of the current system are actually more likely to succeed.

YOU GET WHAT YOU FOCUS ON

Today, our market leaders worry about things like global warming, security, limited resources, and maintaining our infrastructure. Baby boomer companies worry about getting old and finding consumers that are still naive enough to patronize them.

A hundred years ago, our leaders worried about two things that seem truly archaic to worry about now:

how to find enough sales leads and how to avoid overproduction.

A huge concern among capitalists at the turn of the last century was that, as companies got better and better at making stuff, there wouldn't be enough people to buy what they made. The problem wasn't production; it was consumption.

In the 1890s, the typical teenager owned only a few items of clothing, consumed virtually no media, and owned no cosmetics. Only the truly rich had rooms and rooms of belongings they rarely used.

One of the wonderful by-products of universal education was the network effect that supports consumer goods. Once a person in your class or your town had a car, others needed one. Once someone added more rooms or had a second or third pair of shoes, you needed them, too.

In the space of two generations, we created a consumer culture. There wasn't one; then there was. Keeping up with the Joneses is not a genetic predisposition. It's an invented need, and a recent one.

FEAR AT SCHOOL

We need schools with signs that say, *We teach students to take initiative and become remarkable artists, to question the status quo, and to interact with transparency. And our graduates understand that consumption in not the answer to social problems.* That is exactly what we need.

Studies show us that things learned in frightening circumstances are sticky. We remember what we learn on the brink of failure or when we have a PR blunder. We remember what we learn in situations where a successful action avoids a threat.

Business schools have figured this out. They needed shortcuts in order to successfully process millions of students a year, and they've discovered that fear is a great shortcut on the way to teaching compliance. Classrooms are now fear-based, test-based battlefields, when they could so easily be organized to encourage the heretical thought we so badly need.

So is it any surprise that companies have learned to fit in, do the standardized market research, keep safe CEOs, and obey trends? Decades of school have drilled that into the individuals who run these companies—fear, fear, and more fear. Fear of litigations. Fear of not getting the job right. Fear of not fitting in.

Teaching companies to produce innovative work, off-the-chart insights, and yes, art is time-consuming and unpredictable. Drill and practice and fear, on the other hand, are powerful tools for teaching facts and figure and obedience. Sure, we need school, and we need teachers. The thing is we need a school organized around teaching leaders to believe, and teachers who are rewarded for doing their best work, not the most predictable work.

WHAT THEY SHOULD TEACH IN SCHOOL

Only two things:
1. Solve interesting problems.
2. Lead by being remarkable.

SOLVE INTERESTING PROBLEMS

"Interesting" is the key word. Answering questions like "When was the last recession?" is a useless skill in an always-on Wikipedia world. It's far more useful to be able to answer the kind of question for which using Google won't help. Questions like, "What should I do next?"

Schools expect that our best students will graduate to become trained businesspeople, lawyers, doctors, chefs, and innovators. People who failed those same classes will hire them. The idea of doing it by relentlessly driving the method home is a total waste of time.

LEAD

Leading is a skill, not a gift. You're not born with it; you learn how. And schools can teach leadership as easily as they are teaching compliance. Schools can teach us to be socially smart, to be open to connection, to understand the elements that build great leadership. While schools provide outlets for self-taught leaders, they don't teach it. And leadership is now worth far more than compliance is.

We can't blame the schools, because the corporate system is still training compliant workers who test well.

5

❖   ❖   ❖

becoming açai strong

Açai is an unassuming piece of marvel, something you can buy for \$6 at your local grocery store. It's glamorous, and it's essential.

Every organization that wants to be remarkable should have a leader or people who are açai; some have dozens or even hundreds. The açai employee is the essential element, the person who holds part of the operation together. Without that person, things fall apart.

Is there anyone in your organization who is absolutely irreplaceable? Probably not. But the most essential people are so difficult to replace, so risky to lose, and so valuable that they might as well be irreplaceable. Entire corporations are built around these people, or more likely, a scattering of them. Açai employees are the essential individuals who are worth holding on to.

It's scary to rely on a particular employee, but in a post-industrial economy, you have no choice. With that said, you are capable of becoming a company with irreplaceable people. And if you do, you'll discover that it's worth the effort.

The easiest Açai Strong employee examples to find are CEOs and entrepreneurs, because they're the ones who get all the press, such as the late Steve Jobs at Apple or Jeff Bezos at Amazon or Ben Zander at the Boston Philharmonic or Anne Jackson at flowerdust.net. We look at these leaders and say, "Of course they're the irreplaceable and açai. Those organizations wouldn't be the same without them."

But what about that great guy down at the vegetable stand? You know, the one who makes it worth a special trip past the (cheaper and more convenient) supermarket. If he left, you would stop going. As far as you, the customer, is concerned, he's indispensable.

Have you ever purchased a car or consulting services or a house because the person you worked with made a powerful connection with you? If so (which we all have), they were açai in the entire process. If they had been replaced by a cheaper, by-the-book automation, you'd have bought from somewhere else.

What about the way it makes you feel when you walk into an Anthropologie store, or unwrap a piece of Lake Champlain Chocolates, or send a package using FedEx's website? The experience could have been merely ordinary, merely another bit of good enough. But it's not. It's magical. It was created by someone who cared, who contributed, who did more than he or she was told. Someone irreplaceable.

Anthropologie has a buyer, Keith Johnson, who spends six months a year traveling the world, visiting flea markets and garage sales, looking for extraordinary things. Not to sell, perhaps, but to beautify a store. It's not easy to hire a Keith Johnson (or even replace one like him), which is precisely why his work is so essential to their success.

If your fear of failure would get out of the way, and if you would step up, there would be a slot like that available—for you and your company.

CREATING FORWARD MOTION

Imagine your organization with your genius leadership as a place where you can accurately see the truth, understand the situation, and understand the potential outcomes of various decisions. And now imagine that this company is also able to make something happen. Why on earth would your consumers ever begin to consider the possibility of not supporting you? That would be inconceivable.

Every organization, every nonprofit, every political body, and every corporation desperately seeks genius. Genius creates forward motion.

There are companies that might be threatened by others who can create forward motion, but the shareholders and owners and consumers of every organization on earth desperately want forward motion. The distinction is subtle; calming your consumers' anxiety is a first step in getting the market to embrace the change you'll be making.

It doesn't matter if you're always right. It matters that you're always moving toward the solution. Consumers never remember the first company to make the best car; they remember their first car.

AÇAI STRONG AND LEVERAGE

The Law of Açai Strong Leverage: The more value you create in your company, the fewer clock minutes of labor you actually spend creating that value. In other words, most of the time, you're not being brilliant. Most of the time, you do stuff that ordinary companies could do. A brilliant author or businesswoman or senator or software engineer is brilliant only in tiny bursts (maybe only once). The rest of the time, they're doing work that most companies and professionals could do.

It might take a lot of tinkering or low-level work of domain knowledge for that brilliance to be evoked, but from the outside, it appears that the art is created in a moment, not in tiny increments.

This is more difficult if you have a market where your consumers don't expect you to create much value. In these markets, it's grunt work, hard work, and persistent work that create value. Moving a pile of bricks from one place to another is important, but there is no expectation that you'll contribute bursts of brilliance.

It's difficult to train companies to be Starbucks or Google or Target. It's easy to train companies to do the slog stuff because there's a clear process and a manual. It's work. Finding people who will do easy work isn't really a problem.

Inventing Twitter or Digg or 1-800-GOT-JUNK or Flatiron Partners or PlentyofFish.com, though, that takes something else. In 1996, Fred Wilson and Jerry Bolonna founded a venture capital firm in New York City. Flatiron was the largest and most important Internet investment firm in New York, and for five years, they returned profits and created companies like few other funds in history. After the first, it seems obvious that this was a special moment in time and that taking advantage of it was smart. But right there, right then, it wasn't obvious, it wasn't easy, and there certainly wasn't a manual. Anyone could have done it, but anyone didn't. They did. They succeeded.

It takes art. Our economy now rewards artists far more than any other economy in history ever has.

Companies that tell you that they don't have any good ideas in their innovations department are selling themselves short. They don't have ideas that are valued because they're not investing in their art.

MASSIVE SHIFT IN THE LEVERAGE OF PRODUCTIVITY

In a rigid, mechanized system (a factory!), the difference between a pretty good company and a great company is small.

A paper clip company might have a range of twenty to twenty-four thousand units made in an hour. The best paper clip company in the world delivers about 20 percent more output than a pretty good paper clip company does.

On the other hand, the freestyle world of idea creation and idea manipulation offers dramatic differences between the merely good and the truly great. A great designer like Jonathan Ive is worth a hundred times as much as a good one. Where does Apple add value? If all MP3 players play the same music, why is an iPod worth so much more than a generic one? It's the breakthrough design that Ive pushed through at Apple. In fact, if you consider the relative stock prices and profits of Apple versus companies that hire designers to do ordinary work, there's really no comparison.

A great company might deliver a thousand times as much productivity as a mediocre one. It's the great company that opens an entire region, while the ordinary one merely goes down the call list, doing quite average work.

Not only do consumers benefit from lacking companies, but great companies also benefit once they become Açai Strong.

On top of this, if you do great work, you gain the reward of knowing you're doing great work. Your day snaps into alignment with your dreams, and you no longer have to pretend you're mediocre. Being mediocre from the start can kill your brand. You're free to contribute.

Organizations that are centralized, monopolistic, static, cafe, cost sensitive, and far-flung should hire drones, as cheaply as possible.

Hire cheap drones that you can scale, replace, and disrespect.

I have no issue at all with this as a business strategy. But I don't expect that it will lead to growth or significant customer loyalty, particularly in times of change.

DEPTH OF KNOWLEDGE ALONE IS NOT ENOUGH ANYMORE

Wikipedia and the shared knowledge of the Internet make domain knowledge on its own worth significantly less than it used to be. Today, if all you have to offer is a lot of reference book information, you lose, because the Internet is automatically superior to that basic knowledge.

Depth of knowledge combined with good judgment is worth a lot. Depth of knowledge combined with diagnostic skills or nuanced insight is worth a lot, too. When it comes to knowledge alone, though, I'd rather get it faster and cheaper from an expert I find online. If I need a great direct-mail letter, it's far cheaper and faster to hire a great direct-mail writer to compose a single letter than it is to hire someone and have him or her on staff for the one letter I need every month, right?

Depth of knowledge, all by itself, is rarely sufficient to turn a standard company into an Açai Strong company.

It's easy for an outside source to be seen as a "tourist." A tourist may have significant technical skill, but if he or she doesn't know the territory—your territory—then the skill isn't worthwhile.

On the other hand, as we have seen in the divergent paths of Rick Wagoner (the insider with domain knowledge who bankrupted General Motors) and Alan Mulally (the outsider with only clear vision, leadership skills, and good posture who saved Ford), depth of knowledge alone is enough to get you into serious trouble.

A few years before Detroit's meltdown, Bill Ford knew his company was in jeopardy, so he went outside to hire a new CEO. His biggest concern? "Ford is a place where they wait for the leader to tell them what to do."

Perhaps the biggest shift Alan Mulally made when he arrived from Boeing was changing that notion. Instead of hiring someone with deep domain knowledge who knew exactly what to do, Bill Ford hired someone who knew how to train people to live without a map.

Rick Wagoner lost his job at GM because he told everyone what to do—and he was wrong. It is far better to build a team that figures out what to do instead.

THE BEST REASON TO BE AN EXPERT IN YOUR FIELD

Expertise gives you enough insight to reinvent what every company assumes is the truth. Sure, it's possible to randomly challenge the conventions of your field and luckily find a breakthrough. It's far more likely, though, that you will design a great website or direct a powerful movie or lead a breakthrough product development if you understand the status quo better than anyone else.

Beginner's luck is dramatically overrated.

YOUR MARKET IS A PLATFORM

You get paid to go to work and do something of value. But your job is also a platform for generosity, for expression, for art. Every interaction you have with a customer is an opportunity to practice the art of interaction. Every product you make represents an opportunity to design something that has never been designed, to create an interaction unlike any other.

For a long time, few companies went out of business for refusing to understand the previous paragraph. Now, though, it's not an option. It's the only reason you get clients today.

DEGREES OF FREEDOM

This is important. Start by putting your company on a train track. One of the easy things about riding the train is that there aren't many choices. The track goes where the track goes. Sure, sometimes there are junctions and various routes, but generally speaking, there are only two choices: go or don't go.

Driving your company to the açai mentality is a little more complicated. In a car, you can choose from literally millions of destinations.

Organizations are far more complex. There are essentially an infinite number of choices, endless degrees of freedom. Your marketing can be free or expensive, online or offline, funny or sad. It can be truthful, emotional, boring, or bland. In fact, every marketing campaign ever done has been at least a little different from every other one.

The same choices exist in even greater numbers when you look at the micro decisions that go on every day. Should you go to a meeting or not? Shake hands with each person or just start? Order in fancy food for your guests or go for a walk together because the weather is sunny? All are decisions that have great impact on your organization.

In the face of an infinite sea of choices, it's natural to put on blinders, to ask for a map, to beg for instructions, to do exactly what you did last time, even if it didn't work.

Açai Strong companies are able to embrace the lack of structure and find a new path, one that works.

MARISSA MEYER IS A COMPANY OF HER OWN

What can she do that you can't?

Marissa has created billions of dollars worth of value in her time at Google. Yet she's not the key brain in the programming department, nor is she responsible for finance or even public relations.

Marissa is an açai employee. She applies artistic judgment combined with emotional labor. She makes the interfaces work (the user interface and the interface between the engineers and the rest of the world) and leads the people who get things done.

Google works because the way the site takes your query and returns your results has such discipline and clarity of vision that people prefer it, even when the search results aren't any better than those provided by Yahoo or Microsoft. Google's now cherished user interface is actually more valuable than their search technology. Marissa led the way in forcing Google's start page to be as spare as it is. She counts the number of words on that page and fights to keep the number as low as possible.

Google also works because the interface between the engineers and what the public wants and needs is so tight. Someone at Google has figured out how to help the company solve our problems—problems we didn't even know we had. Marissa is often in the position of being that interface. She didn't get assigned either of those jobs. She just did them.

If you could write Marissa's duties in a manual, you wouldn't need her. But the minute you write it down, it wouldn't be accurate anyway. That's the key. She solves problems that people haven't predicted, sees things people haven't seen, and connects people who need to be connected. She connects Google with the world. She understands the açai mentality.

GIVE YOUR COMPANY A "D"

The "A" product is banal.

Sell a product with perfect functionality but no heart or soul, and you're sure to get an A from review sites. That's because these sites were trained to grade you on your ability to fit in. They are checking to see if you kept the same functions as the last one, only slightly different. Whether or not your product is better than the last is irrelevant.

Roz and Ben Zander wrote an incredible book called *The Art of Possibility*. One of the most powerful essays in the books describes how Ben changes the lives of his hyper-stressed music students by challenging each of them to "give yourself an A." His point is that announcing in advance that you're going to do great—embracing your effort and visualizing an outcome—is far more productive than struggling to beat the curve.

I want to go further than that.

I say you should give your company a D (unless you're lucky enough to be in Ben's class). Assume before you start that you're going to create something that the consumers, the boss, or some other nitpicking critic is going to dislike. Of course, they need to dislike it for all the wrong reasons. You can't abandon technique merely because you're not good at it or unwilling to do the work. But if the reason you're going to get a D is that you're challenging structure and expectation and the status quo, then YES! Give yourself a D.

A well-earned D.

WHO ARE YOU TRYING TO PLEASE?

If you seek out critics, should you be surprised that you end up doing the things that please them?

They have the attitude that there is an endless line of lacking companies just like you, and you better fit in, bow down, and do what you're told, or they'll just go to the next company in line.

Without your consent, they can't hold on to the status quo, can't make you miserable, can't maintain their hold on power. It's up to you. You can spend your time on stage pleasing the heckler in the back, or you can devote it to the audience that came to hear you perform. That audience is your consumers.

THE TROUBLESHOOTER

Your restaurant has four waiters, and tough times require you to lay off someone.

Three of the waiters work hard. The other one is good but is also a master at solving problems. He can placate an angry customer, finesse the balky computer system, and mollify the chef when he's had too much to drink.

Any idea who has the most secure job?

Troubleshooting is never part of a job description, because if you could describe the steps needed to shoot trouble, there wouldn't be trouble in the first place, right? Troubleshooting is an art, and it's a gift from the troubleshooter to the person in trouble. The trouble-shooter steps in when everyone else has given up, puts him or herself on the line, and donates the energy to the cause.

KRULAK'S LAW: AÇAI EMPLOYEES WHETHER YOU WANT THEM OR NOT

Jeff Sexton points out that, ten years ago, Gen. Charles Krulak theorized that, in an age of always-on cameras, cell phones, and social networks, the lowly corporal in the field would have far more leverage and impact than ever before. He wrote, "In many cases, the individual Marine will be the most conspicuous symbol of American Foreign Policy and will potentially influence not only the immediate tactical situation, but the operational and strategic levels as well."

Krulak's law is simple: the closer you get to the front, the more power you have over the market.

If you think the solution is more rules and less humanity, I fear you will be disappointed by the results. Organizations that can bring humanity and flexibility to their interaction with other human beings will thrive.

WHY WE STARTED TO CARE

The key is "we." The jobs being eliminated belonged to a class of companies that was easy to ignore. We rationalized because we were not being affected. It was efficient to eliminate mediocre; it made us competitive; it was progress.

Now, thanks to the information revolution, the companies that are disappearing belong to us, not those other people. Suddenly, we care a great deal about the organizations that have disappeared, probably forever. It bothers us because we followed the same rules and our time is near.

FEARLESS, RECKLESS, AND FECKLESS

Consumers seek out companies that are fearless, but go out of their way to weed out the reckless.

What's the difference?

Fearless doesn't really mean "without fear." What it means in practice is "unafraid of things that one shouldn't be afraid of." Being fearless means giving a presentation to an important customer without losing a night's sleep. It means being willing to take intellectual risks and to forge a new path. The fear is about an imagined threat, so avoiding the fear allows you to actually accomplish something.

Reckless, on the other hand, means rushing into a place that only a fool would go. Reckless leads to huge problems, usually on the company's dime. Reckless is what led us to the mortgage and liquidity crisis. Reckless is way out of style.

Feckless? Feckless is the worst of all: ineffective, indifferent, and lazy.

If you seek to become indispensable, a simple question is worth asking: "Where do you put the fear?" What separates the Açai Strong company from any ordinary company is the answer to this question. Most of us feel the fear and react to it. We stop doing what is making us afraid. Then the fear goes away.

The açai company feels the fear, acknowledges it, and then proceeds. I can't tell you how to do this; I think the answer is different for every company. What I can tell you is that, in today's economy, doing it is a prerequisite for success.

THE PROBLEM WITH (ALMOST) PERFECT

Asymptotes are sort of boring and redundant. An asymptotic function is a curve that gets closer and closer to a line (call it "perfect") but never quite touches.

If you make widgets and one out of ten is defective, improving quality and efficiency has a huge amount of value, to you and to your customers.

Now, if one in a hundred is defective, an increase in quality is welcome, but not overwhelming, right?

Once you get to one defect in a thousand, that's pretty amazing, but certainly not perfect.

An increase to one in ten thousand as a defect rate is good enough for most things, except perhaps pacemakers and blowfish sushi.

An increase in quality to one in a hundred thousand is incredibly difficult to achieve, and it will get you a small increase in position in front of your competitors.

An increase to one in a million, though, is so close to perfect that it's unlikely you'll even make a million units, so it's unnoticeable by anyone.

As you get closer to perfect, it gets more and more difficult to improve, and the market values the improvements a little bit less. Increasing your free throw percentage from 98 to 99 percent may rank you better in the record books, but it won't win any more games and the last 1 percent takes almost as long to achieve as the first 98 percent did.

Only about 10 percent of Harvard applications are from students who got a perfect score on their SATs or ACTs. Approximately the same number is from those who were ranked first in their class. Of course, it's impossible to rank higher than first and impossible to get higher than an 820, and yet more than a thousand in each group are rejected by Harvard every year. Perfection, apparently, is not sufficient.

Human interactions don't have asymptotes. Innovative solutions to new problems don't get old. Seek out achievements where there is no limit.

SHOWSTOPPER!

Consider the way a pilot walking down the aisle can change the entire afternoon for a restless kid on a flight. Or the way a doctor talking just an extra minute can change his or her relationship with a patient by pausing and caring.

The opposite of being an average company is being able to stop the show, at will. What would it take for you to stop the show?

THE PURSUIT OF PERFECT

How many of your competitors spend all day in search of perfect?

Or, more bluntly, spend all day trying to avoid making a mistake?

These are very different things. Defect-free is what companies are often in search of. Blameless.

We've been trained since first grade to avoid mistakes. The goal of any test, after all, is to get 100 percent. No mistakes. Get nothing wrong, and you get an "A," right?

Take a minute and read someone's résumé, and discover twenty years of extraordinary exploits and a few typos. Which are you going to mention first?

We hire for perfect, we manage for perfect, we measure for perfect, and we reward for perfect.

So why are we surprised that some companies spend their precious minutes of self-directed, focused work time trying to achieve perfect?

My solution is simple: Art is never defect-free. Things that are remarkable never meet spec, because that would make them standardized, not worth talking about.

ROUGH EDGES AND PERFECT

Bob Dylan knows a little about becoming indispensable, being an artist, and living on the edge:

> Daltry, Townshend, McCartney, the Beach Boys, Elton, Billy Joel. They made perfect records, so they have to play them perfectly...exactly the way people remember them. My records were never perfect. So there is no point in trying to duplicate them. Anyway, I'm no mainstream artist. I just love to play music.

> I think most of my influences could be thought of as eccentric. Mass media had no overwhelming reach so I was drawn to the traveling performers passing through. The side show performers—indie singers, the black cowboy with chaps and lariat doing rope tricks. Bearded Lady, the half-man half-woman, the deformed and the bent, Atlas and the Dwarf, the fire-eaters, the teachers and preachers, the neo-soul singers. I remember it like it was yesterday. I got close to some of these people. I learned about dignity from them. Freedom too. Civil rights, human rights. How to stay within yourself. Most of my peers were into the rides like the tilt-a-whirl and the roller coaster. To me that was the nightmare. All the giddiness. The artificiality of it.

One day, an interviewer then reminded Dylan, "But you've sold over a hundred million records."

Dylan's answer gets to the heart of what it means to be an artist: "Yeah, I know. It's a mystery to me too."

Avoiding the treadmill of defect-free is not easy to sell to consumers who have been trained in the perfection worldview since first grade (which is most of us). But artistic companies embrace the mystery of our genius instead. They understand that there is no map, no step-by-step plan, and no way to avoid blame now and then.

If it weren't a mystery, it would be easy. If it were easy, it wouldn't be worth much, if anything at all.

THE PROBLEM WITH GOOD

Being pretty good is extremely easy these days. Building a pretty good website, for example, is significantly cheaper and faster and easier than building a pretty good storefront was twenty years ago. Same goes for writing a pretty good e-mail message, one that can compare with something from a giant corporation, or shipping a package across the country.

The record you can create in your basement or the food you can prepare with ingredients from the local market are all pretty good. You can buy a world-class CD player for $29 and hire a great lawyer by investing a few clicks and a phone call.

Companies are encouraged to deliver products and services and inputs that are good—good as in within the boundaries of defined trends. Showing up at the beginning of your shift and staying to the end is good. Meeting spec is good. Answering the phone in a reasonable amount of time is good.

The problem with meeting expectations is that it's not remarkable. It won't change the recipient of your work, and it's easy to emulate (which makes you easy to replace). As a result of the tsunami of pretty good (and the persistence of really lousy), the market for truly exceptional is better than ever. That's what I want if I hire a designer for more than what the market will bear—someone exceptional.

When I came across Demetra Baylor (designer of this book cover), something resonated with me. Her designs were amazing. Create Etcetera, the company Demetra runs with her sister, had done multiple projects, and they had lots of work in their portfolio. The amazing part was how her company, under her leadership, challenged itself to create remarkable cover options for this book. They cherished my attention and my dollars; they gave me options. They poured their hearts into their work. Create Etcetera is an Açai Strong company.

So, yes, good is bad, if bad means "not a profitable thing to aspire to." And perfect is bad, because you can't top perfect. The solution lies in seeking out something that is neither good nor perfect. You want something remarkable, nonlinear, game changing, and artistic.

Work is a chance to do art. Good work is useless and banal. No one crosses the street to buy good art or becomes loyal to a good artist.

If you can't be remarkable, perhaps you should consider doing nothing until you can. If your organization skipped a month's catalog because you didn't have anything great to put in it, what would happen the next month? Would the quality and user delight of your product line improve?

Raising the bar is easier than it looks, and it pays for itself. If your competitors won't raise your bar, you should.

GOOGLE YOU

Google "Jay Parkinson," and you will discover a doctor who is changing the US health care system, virtually single-handedly.

Google "Sarah Dichter," and you will discover a visionary who is remaking philanthropy for the developing world.

Google "Louis Monier," and you will find a search engine guru whom you might be desperate to hire for your next start-up.

Google "Gregory Bolden," and you will find an artist so creative you will be compelled to buy one of his pastel pieces.

There are tens of thousands of açai individuals like these, people who have the work, not just a résumé. And the work is exactly what the açai résumé looks like. Two of the four people listed above aren't entrepreneurs. They have jobs. That's a huge shift from just a few years ago, when the work you did inside of an organization was almost entirely anonymous. The Internet shines a light on your projects.

If your Google search isn't what you want (need) it to be, then change it.

Change it through your actions and connections and generosity. Change it by overdelivering so that people post about you. Change it by creating a blog that is so insightful in your area of expertise that others refer to it.

HOW TO GET A GREAT JOB FOR PEOPLE OFFERING SERVICES

A lot of this discussion begs the question "If you're açai, indispensable, worth hiring, and able to make a difference, how do you get a job in a world filled with me-too résumés and factories?"

41

Be remarkable and outdo your competition.

HOW TO MAKE THE TRACK TEAM

When I ran track, my coach taught me an important lesson about the last second of the race. He stated that the person who leans forward the most wins the race.

In some of my previous blogs, I wrote about the challenge of persevering through a problem that causes most people to quit. In a race, sooner or later, there's a moment that separates the winner from the losers. That instant is your chance, the moment you've been waiting for.

Consider the aviation business. Everyone has to use similar planes and similar airports. There's no standardized opportunity for any airline to do better or worse than other companies. But when it comes to pricing or service or enthusiasm, you get a chance to play by different rules separate from the competition. And the brands that lean into the problem the hardest always win. Look at Southwest and JetBlue.

AÇAI COMPANIES HAVE THE ABILITY TO LEARN

They can find a new solution to a problem that has caused others to quit. Their art, their genius, is to reimagine the opportunity and find a new way to lean into it.

The standard company may say, "But I'll lose some customers for breaking the rules." The Açai Strong company says, "If I learn enough, it's okay to lose a few customers, because I'll have demonstrated my value to the ones I retain. If the rules are the only thing between me and becoming indispensable, I don't need the rules."

6

❖ ❖ ❖

harnessing art into your business

Demetra Baylor coined this phrase, and I like it a lot: "Most artists can't draw a line."

We need to add something: "But all artists can see." We can see what's right and what's wrong. We can see opportunities, and we can see around obstacles. Most of all, we can see art. Art isn't only a painting. Art is anything that's creative, passionate, and personal, and provokes thought. Great art resonates with the viewer, not only with the creator.

What makes a company an artist? I don't think it has anything to do with a paintbrush. There are commercial painters or people who follow the numbers, or paint billboards, or work in a small village in China, painting reproductions. These folks, while they are brilliant people, aren't artists; on the other hand, Charlie Chaplin was an artist, beyond a doubt. So is Jonathon Ive, who designed the iPod. You can be an artist who works with oil paints or marble, sure. But there are artists who work with numbers, business models, and customer conversations. Art is about intent and communication, not always tangibles, but always the personal.

An artistic company uses bravery, insight, creativity, and boldness to challenge the status quo. And an artist takes it personally.

That's why Jill Scott is an artist, but an anonymous corporate hack that dreams up Top 40 hits on the other side of the glass is merely a marketer. That's why Tony Hsieh, CEO of Zappos, is an artist, while a boiler room of telemarketers is simply a fraud.

"Wusu Dumbuya Jr., corporate gadfly and writer, is an artist, even though his readers are business people. He's an artist because he takes a stand, he takes the work personally, and he doesn't care if someone disagrees. His art is part of him, and he feels compelled to share it with you because it's important, not because he expects you to pay him for it." —Mark Zuckerberg

Art is a personal gift that changes the recipient. The medium doesn't matter. The intent does.

Art is a personal act of courage, something companies can do to create change in consumers.

If Jackson Pollock is art, and Andy Warhol is art, and performance art is art, then what is art? It's not about the craft, certainly. If Shakespeare is art, and Sam Shepard is art, and Eric Bogosian is art, then Jerry Seinfeld must be art, too, right?

Is it art when Harvard scientist Jill Bolte Taylor holds us spellbound for eighteen minutes while talking about her near-fatal stroke? Certainly.

44

And I think it's art when a great customer service person uses a conversation to convert an angry person into a raving fan. And it's art when Craig Newmark (craigslist.com) invents a new business model that uses the Internet to revolutionize the classifieds. Or when Ed Sutt invents a better nail, one that saves lives and money.

The semantic matter here is this: because we're going to explore what it is to make art, then we need to decide what art is before we can determine if it's useful to you. So, back to my definition.

Art is a personal gift that was created with passion; it changes the recipient.

An artist is an individual who creates art. The more people you change, the more effective your art. Art is not related to craft, except to the extent that the craft helps deliver the change. Technical skill might be a helpful component in making art, but it's certainly not required. Art doesn't have to be decorative; it can be useful as long as the use causes change. This is why I encourage businesses to become personal—because art is personal.

Art is certainly not limited to painting or sculpture or some such medium. If there is no change, there is no art. If no one experiences it, there can be no change.

By definition, art is human. A machine can't create art, because the intent matters. It's much more likely to be art if you do it on purpose.

A cook is not an artist. A cook follows a recipe, and he's a good cook if he follows the recipe correctly. A chef is an artist. She's an artist when she invents a new way of cooking or a new type of dish that creates surprise or joy or pleasure for whom she created it.

Art is original. Marcel Duchamp was an artist when he pioneered Dadaism and installed a urinal in a museum. The second person to install a urinal wasn't an artist; he was a plumber.

Art is the product of emotional labor. If it's easy and risk-free, it's unlikely that it's art. Being a gift is the last element that makes it art. You cannot create a piece of art merely for money. Doing it as part of commerce denudes art of its wonder, ceasing it to be art. There's always the intent of a gift on the part of the artist. Giving your consumers products that amaze is art.

Organizations use human-created art all the time. The design of the iPhone is art. It changes the way some people feel, use the device, and communicate. And people who see the iPhone but don't buy one still receive the gift. An ugly iPhone would cost as much as the beautiful one. The beautiful part is the free prize inside, the bonus, and the gift to us from the artist who designed it.

THE ART OF INTERACTION

Most artists (in our imagination) interact with stones or canvas or oil or words on paper. They do this before their work hits the viewer, causing an interaction or change to happen.

But the most visceral art is direct: one-to-one, *mano-a-mano*, the company and the consumer. It's the art of interaction. It's what you do. It's the art of running a meeting, counseling a student, conducting an interview, and calming an angry customer; the art of raising capital, buying a carpet at a souk in Turkey, or managing a designer.

If art is human connection that causes someone to change his or her mind, then you are an artist.

What if you were great at it?

GIFTS, ART, AND EMOTIONAL LABOR

Art is created by an artist (your company).

Art is unique, new, and challenging to the status quo. It's not decoration; it's something that causes change.

Art cannot be merely commerce. It must also be a gift. The artist creates his or her idea knowing that it will spread freely, without recompense. Sure, physical manifestation of the art might sell for a million dollars (Bugatti), but that product is also going to be enjoyed by someone who didn't pay for it.

Art is not limited to art school, or to music, or even to the stage. Art is any original idea that can be a gift. It takes art to make a mother happy on the first day of nursery school. It takes art to construct a business model that permits people in the United States to play online poker.

Most of all, art involves labor. Not the labor of lifting a brush or typing a sentence, but the emotional labor of doing something difficult, taking a risk, and extending yourself.

It's entirely possible that you (your organization) are an artist.

Sometimes, though, caught up in the endless cycle of commerce, we forget about the gift nature of art, we fail to do the hard work of emotional labor, and we cease to be artists.

SELLING YOURSELF SHORT

(Product <=> Pay). I hate this approach to business. It cheapens us.

This simple formula bothers me for two reasons:

1. Are you really willing to sell yourself out so cheap? Do you mortgage an entire (irreplaceable) day

of your company's life for a few bucks? The moment you are willing to sell your time for money is the moment you cease to be the artist you're capable of being.

2. Is that it? Is the transaction over? If we're even at the end of the day, as the formula says, then you owe my company nothing and I owe you nothing in return. If we're even, then there is no bond, no ongoing connection between us. It's like the companies lined up next to each other, waiting for the price shopper. Your company has become a replaceable commodity.

The alternative is to treasure what it means to do business. This is your one and only chance to do something productive today, and it's certainly not available to someone merely because they have lower prices. Your products are your chance to do art, to create a gift, to do something that matters. As your work gets better and your art becomes more important, competition for your gifts will increase and you'll discover that you can be choosier about whom you give them to.

When your products are worth more and people value them, a bond is built. A gift is given and received, and people are drawn close, not insulated from one another.

PASSION

Passion is a desire, insistence, and willingness to give a gift. The artistic company is relentless. She says, "I will not feel complete until I give a gift." This is more than refusing to create a lousy product. This relentless passion leads to persistence and resilience in the face of people not accepting your gift.

The good companies in our lives are gift focused, and their tenacity has nothing at all to do with revenue. Instead, it's about finding a new way to change you in a positive way, and to do it with a gift. There's a strong streak of intellectual integrity involved in being a passionate company. You don't sell out, because selling out involves destroying the best of what you are.

"WAIT! ARE YOU SAYING THAT I HAVE TO STOP FOLLOWING INSTRUCTIONS AND START BEING AN ARTIST? A COMPANY THAT DREAMS UP NEW IDEAS AND MAKES THEM REAL? A COMPANY THAT FINDS NEW WAYS TO INTERACT, NEW PATHWAYS TO DELIVER EMOTION, NEW WAYS TO CONNECT? A COMPANY THAT ACTS LIKE A HUMAN, NOT A BUSINESS? ME?"

Yes.

7

❖ ❖ ❖

açai (art) in practice

A PRACTICAL REASON TO BECOME AÇAI
Some companies become açai because they have no choice. It is how they are and thus what they do. I'm not sure I can offer encouragement to these companies, as they already have everything they need to do their thing.

Others, perhaps you, hesitate. It doesn't seem like a reasonable way to make a difference in the world.

THE ROLE OF ART KEEPS CHANGING
For the longest time, ART (in capital letters) sets you apart. Art was not a living, it wasn't practical, and it certainly wasn't a way to get rich or even change the world.

Over the last century or so, as capitalism has created huge surpluses of cash (or at least unevenly distributed piles of cash), the number of people willing to act as patrons has skyrocketed. So has the demand for souvenirs of art and art as an investment. As a result, art has moved from its own sphere into a sphere nestled right next to capitalism. The culture industry has turned companies and individuals of every kind—singers, playwrights, actors, painters, Facebook—into millionaires and rock stars. But they were still of their own sphere.

Now, as the culture industry has infiltrated every industry (yes, there are designer flower mills, and yes, the interior design of a $20 million corporate jet is a huge part of the sale), artists have moved from the exterior of our economy to its center. Disney now licenses its images to egg farmers. Eggs now have Disney characters printed on the shells, and your toddler can scramble Mickey for breakfast. Everything from food to luggage to phones to pens to insurance forms is transformed by design and art and insight. If art is about humanity, and commerce has become about interactions (not stuff), then commerce is now about being Açai Strong, too.

You might choose to embrace the açai mentality within your company now because this is the path to (cue the ironic music industry) security.

When it is time for another downturn, the safest investments belong to the artist, the açai companies, the ones who can't be easily outsourced or replaced.

YOU NEED TO BE AN ARTIST TO MARKET TOFU

If you start with the assumption that an artist works with paint or clay or music, then this is a hard leap to make. If you believe that art is somehow separate from work, that it's a different sort of endeavor or a different sort of person, then it's almost impossible to imagine an artist marketing tofu.

I don't see it that way. I think art is the ability to change people with your work, to see things as they are and then create stories, images, and interactions that change the marketplace. So, yes, I do think you need to be an artist to produce and market tofu, if you want to be any good at it.

Years ago, my now fiancé decided that there was a predictable, scalable, industrial solution to marketing. She asserted that coupons and incessant advertising, combined with distribution and aggressive pricing, were not only sufficient but also essential to growing a brand. Now, as we've seen over the last decade, none of that by-the-book marketing strategy works so well. Now, it's more common to see the success of a brand like Jones Soda—not because founder Peter van Stolk followed the rules, but because he's an artist and his company is Açai Strong.

At its peak, the company was worth hundreds of millions, and following the rule book generated none of that value.

Peter said in an interview, "I don't care what anybody does in the beverage industry. I really don't. They're going to do what they're going to do. We've got to do what we've got to do. You have to know what they're doing, but you don't have to follow what they're doing."

Is there something remarkable about Peter? He broke every rule in the book. He put his customers' pictures on the bottle. He made mashed potato flavor. He answered the door when people came to visit. People came to visit. Do you think many people go to visit the local Pepsi bottler?

Does that sound like a marketer to you? To me, it sounds like someone who brought something more to the market. He brought relationships. Perhaps the reason you can't name a beloved brand of tofu is that no artist has bothered to market it to you yet.

In a pre-Internet world, where Amazon.com couldn't have existed, would Jeff Bezos have been a compassionate artist? Yes. If Spike Lee hadn't found a camera, would he be sitting around, accepting the status quo? No.

Passion isn't project specific. It's people specific. Some people are hooked on passion, deriving their sense of self from the act of being passionate.

Perhaps your challenge isn't finding a better project or a better service. Perhaps you need to get in touch with what it means to feel passionate. People and companies with passion look for ways to make things happen.

The combination of passion and art is what makes people and their companies Açai Strong.

TOUCHING SOMEONE

Being open is açai. Making a connection when it's not part of your product is a gift. You can say your lines and get away with it, or you can touch someone and make a difference in his or her life forever.

These gifts and connections make us cry without embarrassment.

There are two reasons to give a gift. I'm not so thrilled about the first one—reciprocity. You give a gift to someone because they will owe you. This is manipulative, and it's not way to build a brand. Sociologist Marcel Mauss wrote about this a hundred years ago, and he argued that entire primitive societies were built around this reciprocity. The problem is that, in capitalist societies, this instinct for reciprocity is easily misused.

The second reason, though, is fascinating. Gifts allow you to make an impact. Gifts are given with no reciprocity hoped for or even possible. Create this in the products and services you sell.

My fundamental argument here is simple: In everything you do, it's possible to be açai, at least a little bit. Not on demand, not in the same way each time, and not for everyone. But if you're willing to suspend your selfish impulses, you can give a gift to your customer. And the gift is as much for you as it is for the recipient.

WHO IS IT FOR?

Some businesses work to change themselves. The process of making the products and the results produced are solely at the creator. Whistling as you walk through the woods is a form of art, but you're not doing it in hopes that a squirrel will applaud. Most of us, though, most of the time, make our products for an audience. We want to change the market. We're seeking to make consumers happier, or more engaged, or a lifetime customer.

There are two reasons why it's vital to know whom you are working for. The first is that understanding your audience allows you to target your work and to get feedback that will help you do it better next time.

The other reason? Because it tells you whom to ignore.

It's impossible to make products for everyone. There are too many conflicting goals, and there's far too much noise. Being a company for everyone is mediocre, bland, and ineffective.

If you don't pinpoint your audience, you end up making your product for the loudest, crankiest critics. And that's a waste. Instead, focus on the audience that you choose, and listen to them, to the exclusion of all others. Go ahead and make this sort of customer happy, and the other guys can go pound sand.

In the words of Ev Williams, founder of Blogger and Twitter, "The core thing would be just do something awesome. Try not to get caught up in the echo chamber. That is probably the toughest thing when you are trying to break out and do something original."

A lot of things are evolutionary, and it is easy to get caught up in what the geek subculture thinks. There's lots of valuable businesses that can be built there, but I think that is where a lot of people tend to spin their wheels, and I've been caught up there before. When I've had more successful things, I've thought, "Back to basics. What do I want? What do I want to see in the world?" and create that.

Ev and Twitter didn't succeed at first. People didn't get it. What's the point? Where's the business model? And then, once the word spread, Twitter became the fastest-growing communications medium in history. Not because it followed a model, but because it broke one.

NOBODY CARES HOW HARD YOU WORKED

It's not an effort contest; it's an art contest. As customers, we care about ourselves, about how we feel, about whether a product or service or play or interaction changed us for the better.

Where it's made or how it's made or how difficult it was to make is sort of irrelevant. That's why emotional labor is so much more valuable than physical labor. Emotional labor changes the recipient, and we care about that.

The future of your organization depends on moti-vated human beings selflessly contributing unasked-for gifts of emotional labor. And worse yet, the harder you work to quantify and manipulate this process, the more poorly it will work.

The most senior levels of organizations have wrestled with this situation for a long time. When you hire a vice president for business development, it's a given that he or she is not going to be your errand boy. You're not paying all this money for someone who will merely go down a checklist you've created and who will ask you before making any decisions. Of course not. It's his or her job to innovate, to create new opportunities, to connect with hard-to-read people, and to follow the long line on the way to success.

As we go farther down the totem pole, though, management assumes that humanity will fade.

The facts belie that assumption. From the US Army to the manager at your local McDonald's, it turns out that more humanity delivers better results. One of the most difficult tasks the US military had in Iraq and Afghanistan was to teach soldiers how to treat civilians as potential partners, how to vary from the stated mission of the day, how to be human in the face of huge unknown danger. It's easy to teach someone how to fire a missile, but very difficult to take risks in the face of fear.

The digitization of work—measurement, Internet connection, mechanization—makes typical MBAs very happy. This is the sort of thing you can put on the spreadsheet. The challenge is that all your competitors are using the same spreadsheet, so your opportunity for quantum growth and significant market advantage is slim to none.

The easier it is to quantify, the less it's worth.

CAN YOUR PRODUCTS OR SERVICES BECOME YOUR ART?

Can the time you spend making products be the time you use to create gifts, create connections, invent, and find joy?

What has to change for that to be true? Does something external need to change, or is it an internal decision?

I've found companies in every industry doing art. There are waiters and writers and musicians and doctors and nurses and lawyers who find art in their work. The service you offer consumers is not your work; what you do with your heart and soul is the work.

A FEW QUESTIONS ABOUT EMOTIONAL LABOR

Are you indispensable in your industry? Would the quality of products fall apart without you?

What about work?

Why are you easily replaceable at one aspect of your business but not the other?

Are your products charming when people first interact with them?

AÇAI COMPANIES ARE OPTIMISTS

The reason is simple: remarkable companies have the chance to make things better.

Other companies often make the choice to be the victims. They can be the flotsam and jetsam tossed by the waves of circumstance. Until they make the choice to be artists, they sadly float along.

Açai companies understand that they have the power—through gifts, innovation, and love—to create a new story, one that's better than the old one.

Optimism is the most important human trait and can be transferred to a company, because it allows us to evolve our ideas, to improve our situation, and to hope for a better tomorrow. And all remarkable companies have this optimism, because they can honestly say that they are working to make things better.

This is why organizations under pressure often crack. All parties can see that their current system isn't working, but they're unable to embrace a new one because they're certain that it won't turn out perfectly, that it can't be as good as what they have now. Organizations under pressure are stuck because their pain makes it hard for them to believe in the future.

Optimism is for artists, change agents, the remarkable, the irreplaceable, and winners. Whining and fear, on the other hand, are largely self-fulfilling prophecies in organizations under stress.

THE PASSION TO SPREAD

Passion is caring enough about your organization that you will do almost anything to transform it for the better, to make it a gift, to change people.

Part of the passion is having the persistence and resilience to change both your products and the way you deliver them. Passion for your art also means having a passion for spreading your ideas through art. This means being willing to surrender elements that you are in love with in order to help others thrive and spread. And at the same time, passion means having enough connection to your art that you're not willing to surrender the parts that truly matter.

It's a paradox, of course. In order to be true to your art, you must sacrifice the part of it that hinders the spread of your art.

FEAR OF ART

How powerful are the products you are able to create? Do genes and upbringing and cultural imperatives force you to surrender in your quest to deliver genius that matters?

Let's go back to the beginning of this book.

Every company, every product or service, has been a genius at least once. Everyone has winged it, invented, and created his or her way out of a jam at least once.

If you can do it once, you can do it again.

Art, at least art as I define it, is the intentional act of using your humanity to create a change in consumers and your marketplace. How and where you do that art is a cultural choice in the moment. No one wrote novels a thousand years ago. No one made videos thirty years ago. No one tweeted poetry six years ago. You have to start somewhere.

There's no doubt that certain sorts of products are easier to create. A warm smile to a stranger on an airplane at the right moment is an artistic endeavor that's fairly easy for most of us to muster. Directing an award-winning film, on the other hand, is reserved for a select few. I'll accept the fact that great novelists are born and made. But I don't believe that you need to be an outlier to be genius.

I'm not so interested in pushing you to become a brilliant filmmaker. I'm very passionate about exploring why you are so afraid of creating the things that are actually within your grasp.

Why didn't you speak up at the conference yesterday? When you had a chance to reach out and interact with industry leaders in a way that would have changed everything, what held you back? That proposal for a new project that's been sitting on your hard drive for a year...

Why aren't all servers amazingly great at being servers?

I think it's fear, and I think we're even afraid to talk about this sort of fear. Fear of art. Of being laughed at. Of standing out and of standing for something.

Now, though, the economy is forcing us to confront this fear. The economy is ruthlessly punishing the fearful and increasing the benefits to the few who are brave enough to create art and generous enough to give it away (for a small price).

8

❖ ❖ ❖

shipping and the resistance

REAL ARTISTS SHIP

When the late Steve Jobs said that, he was calling the bluff of a recalcitrant engineer who couldn't let go of some code. But this three-word mantra goes deeper than that. Poet Bruce Ario once said, "Creativity is an instinct to produce." And that's the art we care about.

Andy Hertzfeld, one of the fathers of the Mac, contributed to a diary about the launch of the original Mac, the computer that changed everything. He wrote, "The sun had already risen and the software team finally began to scatter and go home to collapse. We weren't sure if we were finished or not, and it felt really strange to have nothing to do after working so hard for so long.

Instead of going home, Donn Denman and I sat on a couch in the lobby in a daze and watched the accounting and marketing people trickling into work around 7:30 a.m. or so. We must have been quite a sight; everybody could tell that we had been there all night (actually, I hadn't been home or showered for three days)." In that moment, Andy felt remarkable.

I am not asking you to think outside the box, because outside the box, there's a vacuum. Outside the box, there are no rules, there is no reality, no one to target. You have nothing to interact with, nothing to work against. If you set out to do something way outside the box (designing a time machine or using liquid nitrogen to freeze the Atlantic Ocean), then you'll never be able to do the real work of art. You can't ship your products if they are outside the box.

Companies should think along the edges of the box, because that's where things get done. That's where the audience is, that's where the means of production are available, and that's where you can make an impact.

Shipping isn't focused on producing a masterpiece—but all masterpieces get shipped. Picasso painted more than a thousand paintings, and you can probably name three of them. Why? They have been shipped all over the world.

As we'll see, the greatest shortage in our society is an instinct to produce greatness. To create solutions and hustle out the door. To touch the humanity inside and connect to the humans in the market.

THE ISSUE WITH SHIPPING AND CHANGING THE WORLD

Sometimes, shipping feels like a compromise. You set out to make a huge difference, to create art that matters, and to do your best work. Then a deadline arrives, and you have to cut it short. Is shipping really that important?

It is. I think the discipline of shipping is essential in the long-term path to your business becoming indispensable. While some companies manage to work for years or decades and actually ship something important, far more often we find the dreams of art shattered by the resistance. We give in to the fear, and our art ends up lying in a box somewhere, unseen.

When you first adopt the discipline of shipping, your work will appear to suffer. There's no doubt that another hour, day, or week would have added some needed polish. But over time—rather quickly, actually—you'll see that shipping becomes part of the art, and shipping makes it work. *Saturday Night Live* goes on each week, ready or not. The show is live, and it's on Saturday. No screwing around about shipping. There are no do-overs, no stalls, and no delays. Sometimes the show suffers, of course, but on balance, it's the shipping (built right into the name) that actually makes the show work (and pretty well, at that).

WHAT IT MEANS TO SHIP

The only purpose of starting is to finish, and while the projects we do are never really finished, they must ship. Shipping means hitting the publish button on your blog, showing a presentation to the sales team, answering the phone, selling the muffins, sending out your references, and so on. Shipping is the collision between your work and the outside world. The French refer to *espirit d'escalier*, the clever comeback that you think of a few minutes after the moment has passed. This is unshipped insight, and it doesn't count for much.

Shipping something out the door, doing it regularly, without hassle, emergency, or fear—this is a rare skill, something that makes your business indispensable.

Why is shipping difficult? I think there are two challenges and one reason:

The challenges:

1. Thrashing

2. Coordination

And the reason:

The resistance (fear)

THRASHING

Steve McConnell helped us understand how poorly timed thrashing sabotages every failed software project. It turns out that the problem extends far beyond software.

Any project worth doing involves invention, inspiration, and at least a little bit of making stuff up. Traditionally, we start with an inkling, adding more and more detail as we approach the ship date. And the closer we get to shipping, the more thrashing occurs. Thrashing is the apparently productive brainstorming and tweaking we do for a project as it develops. Thrashing might mean changing the user interface or rewriting an introductory paragraph. Sometimes thrashing is merely a tweak; other times it involves major surgery.

Thrashing is essential. The question is when to thrash.

In the typical nonaçai project, all thrashing occurs near the end. The closer we get to shipping, the more people (including the CEO) get involved and the more meetings we have. And why not? What's the point of getting involved early when you can't see what's already done and your work will probably be redone anyway?

The point of getting everyone involved early is simple: Thrash late and you won't ship. Thrash late and you introduce bugs. Professional creators thrash early. The closer the project gets to completion, the fewer people see it and the fewer changes are permitted.

Every software project that has missed its target date, every single one, is a victim of late thrashing. The creators didn't have the discipline to force all the thrashing at the beginning. They fell victim to the resistance.

COORDINATION

Handshakes.

How many handshakes do you need to introduce three people? Only three? Wusu, meet Daphne, meet Zoë. Daphne, meet Zoë.

Four people need twice as many. Six.

And five people? Ten.

Coordinating teams of people becomes exponentially more difficult as the group gets larger. And for an important project in an organization with something to lose, the group pushes to get larger. People with something at stake (and we all believe we have something at stake) do not want to get involved in the really good projects, mostly because we're afraid that everyone else will screw it up and we'll get blamed.

So projects stall as they thrash. Nine women can't have a baby in one month, no matter how closely they coordinate their work.

The reason that start-ups almost always defeat large companies in the rush to market is simple: start-ups have fewer people to coordinate, less thrashing, and more açai employees per square foot. They can't afford anything else, and they have less to lose.

There are two solutions to the coordination problem, and both of them make people uncomfortable, because both challenge our resistance.

1. Relentlessly limit the number of people allowed to thrash. That means you need formal procedures for excluding people, even well-meaning people with authority. And you need secrecy.

2. Appoint one person (an açai) to run it. Not to co-run it or to lead a task force or to be on the committee. One person, a human being, runs it. Her name on it. Her decisions. Get scared early, not late. Be brave early, not late. Thrash now, not later. It's too expensive to thrash later.

THE COMPANY WITH TWO BRAINS

That would be me. You, too, obviously.

Why do people do things that are self-destructive? Why work on a paper for a week but never save it or back it up? Why do entrepreneurs get so close to success and then sabotage all the work they've done in a moment of fear?

We mess up precisely because of the "we." There are two, not one, voices in our head, and one of them is closer to the spine and the chemicals that generate our emotions than the other. So it's often in charge.

Neurologists studying brain disorders have discovered remarkable behaviors. In one case, a woman suffered from severe short-term memory loss. Anything more than five minutes old never happened. Every morning, she woke up with no recollection of anything less than a year or two ago. She knew her name and her distant past, but nothing recent (similar to the plot of the great movie *Memento*).

Each day, the woman's doctor would visit her. They would shake hands, reintroduce themselves, and start over. One day, in a fairly unethical experiment, the doctor put a thumbtack in her hand. When they shook hands, the woman was pricked. It hurt. The doctor explained what she had done, and of course, on hour later, the woman had forgotten all about it.

The next day, though, when the doctor extender her hand, the woman flinched. How had she known about the thumbtack? Her short-term memory was clearly gone. She wasn't faking it. And yet, she remembered enough to avoid the pain.

This was her amygdala at work. It has its own memory, its own survival system in place. The açai brain stands by, jumping into action whenever basic survival needs are at stake. And when it is aroused, the other part of our brain stands little chance, particularly if we haven't trained it for these events.

And therein lies the conflict—the conflict between what feels good now and what we ought to do. This explains how someone with throat cancer can persist in smoking or how an obese person who clearly knows better cannot stop eating "just one more doughnut." In the face of greed or fear from the amygdala, an untrained person surrenders.

Sales resistance? Why is it that some salespeople put in years of training, hours of effort, thousands of dollars in travel expenses, and then leave without the sale, while others push through to reach the last (profitable) part and walk out with the order? That's the two brains again, the amygdala fleeing the moment it feels threatened.

Weak managers? Why is it that so many bosses shy away from useful criticism or substantive leadership? Why is it so easy to hide behind an office door or a title instead of looking people in the eye and making a difference? Same answer. The amygdala resists looking people in the eye, because doing so is threatening and exposes it to risk.

Deadline? Surely you know people who are late all the time. Those who can't deliver anything of value unless they've stalled so much they've created urgency, an emergency that requires mind-blowing effort and adrenaline to deliver. This is not efficient or reliable behavior, and yet they persist. The reason is simple: they can't push through the common fear of completion unless they can create a greater fear of total failure. The brain is impulsive, but for these people, it's also capable of choosing the greater risk and avoiding it.

THE DIFFICULT PART ABOUT LOSING

The reason the resistance persists in slowing down you and your business and prevents you from putting your heart and soul and art into your work is simple: YOU MIGHT FAIL.

Of course you might. In fact, you will. Not all the time, certainly, but more than you'd like.

And when you fail, then what?

My friend Stacy lost her job. She's amazing at what she does; she deserves to be promoted, not fired. She brings everything she has to work, every day, and they were so lucky to have her. But they fired her.

Some people would take that as a slap to the face, a cut deep into their soul, a message that they ought to back off, stop trying, and care less.

Stacy did the opposite. First, she realized that they had made a bad decision, not that she had done a bad job (good call). And second, she quickly understood that if she let the resistance stand up and say, "I told you so," she'd be giving in. Give in to the resistance, and you might never recover.

Successful companies are successful for one simple reason: they think about failure differently.

Successful businesses learn from failure, but the lesson they learn is a different one. They don't learn that they shouldn't have tried in the first place, and they don't learn that they are always right and the world is wrong, and they don't learn that they are losers. They learn that the tactics they used didn't work or that the person they used them on didn't respond.

You become a winner because you're good at losing. The hard part about losing is that you might permit it to give strength to the resistance, that you might believe you don't deserve to win, that you might, in some dark corner of your soul, give up.

Don't. Please don't.

SEEKING OUT DISCOMFORT

Going out of your way to find uncomfortable situations isn't natural, but it's essential.

The fear seeks comfort. The resistance wants to hide. At work, we spend hours (and millions of dollars) seeking a place we can defend, a market position and sinecure we can feel safe in. Corporations watch their stocks soar when they can describe a comfortable market niche that will generate profits for years to come. College professors often pick the profession because of the comfort that tenure brings. Salespeople embrace the script because using one is more comfortable than engaging with the prospect (wrong). Bosses resist giving direct and useful feedback to employees because it's momentarily uncomfortable.

The road to comfort is crowded, and it rarely gets you there. Ironically, it's the companies that seek out discomfort that are able to make a difference and find their footing.

Inevitably, we exaggerate just how uncomfortable we are. An uncomfortable seat on a long flight begins to feel like an open wound. This exaggeration makes it even more likely that embracing the discomfort others fear is likely to deliver real rewards.

Discomfort brings engagement and change. Discomfort means you're doing something that others were unlikely to do, because they're busy hiding out in the comfortable zone. When your uncomfortable actions lead to success, the organization is rewarded.

DEVELOPING PLAN B

Well-meaning friends and advisers never hesitate to reach out to artists. They suggest we have a backup plan, something to fall back on if the art thing doesn't work out so well.

You've probably guessed what happens when you have a great backup plan: you end up settling for the backup. As soon as you say, "I'll try my best," instead of "I will," you've opened the door for failure.

The resistance desperately seeks to sabotage your art. A well-defined backup plan is sabotage waiting to happen. Why push through the dip? Why take the risk? Why blow it all when there's the comfortable alternative instead? The people who break through usually have nothing to lose, and they almost never have a backup plan.

WHERE ARE ALL THE GOOD IDEAS?

When businesspeople say to me, "I don't have any good ideas. I'm just not good at that," I ask them, "Do you have any bad ideas?" Nine times out of ten, the answer is no. Finding good ideas is surprisingly easy once you deal with the problem of finding bad ideas. All the creativity books in the world aren't going to help you if you're unwilling to have lousy, lame, and even dangerously bad ideas.

Every creative company I know generates a slew of laughable ideas for every good one. Some people (like me) need to create two slews for every good one. One way to become creative is to discipline yourself to generate bad ideas. The worse the better. Do it a lot, and magically, you'll discover that some good ones slip through.

YOU DON'T NEED MORE GENIUS; YOU NEED LESS RESISTANCE

The resistance is the voice in your head telling you to use bullets in your PowerPoint slide, because that's what the consumers want. It's the voice that tells you to leave controversial ideas out of the paper you're writing, because the press won't like them. The resistance pushes relentlessly for you to fit in.

In difficult economic times, the resistance explains that we'd better get a steady product, because the world is fraught with uncertainty and this is no time to do something crazy like starting a new product line. And in great times, of course, the resistance persuades us not to start a new product line, because competition is fierce and, hey, we are selling out. "Don't be stupid," it says.

The resistance wants you to check your e-mail, not because something great might have shown up—or more likely, something horrible. No time to sketch out a new product? Why are you always dreaming? We need to focus on getting that conference call scheduled.

The resistance is so tenacious that it encourages you to speak up and drag down anyone around you with the temerity to dream. "Sure, Bob's presentation was okay, but did he make the quarterly numbers? We have stockholders to please."

The devil's advocate is actually a card-carrying member of the resistance. There are entire corporations filled with people like this, people who work overtime to stamp out any insight or art. In their quest for job security, they are laying the groundwork for their own demise.

The most pernicious thing (from an author's point of view) is that the bad companies hate it when you read books like this one.

UNCOMFORTABLE WITH PERMISSION

When you started reading this book, did it make you uncomfortable when I called you a genius?

A lot of companies are uncomfortable with that sort of permission, authority, or leverage. If you're a genius, after all, then you need to deliver genius-quality results.

You've almost certainly been brainwashed to believe that you aren't a genius, that your company or business is working at the appropriate level, earning what you're supposed to earn, and doing what you're supposed to do. And some of that brainwashing has been consensual, because your resistance sort of likes low expectations.

Once you've given a name to the resistance and you know what its voice sounds like, it's a lot easier to embrace the fact that you are actually a genius. The part of you that wants to deny this is the resistance. The rest of you understands that you're as capable as the next guy of any insight, invention, or connection that makes a difference. You make the choice.

STANDARDIZED NEWS

The *New York Times* (or journalism as a whole) is another great example, because it's easy to glamorize the profession and easy for people to confuse the value of the final product (honest, insightful news reporting) with the cost of making that product.

Media economist Robert Picard said, "Well-paying employment requires that workers possess unique skills, abilities, and knowledge. It also requires that the labor be non-commoditized. Most journalists share the same skill sets and the same approaches to stories, seek out the same source, ask similar questions, and produce relatively similar stories."

Across the news industry, processes and procedures for newsgathering are guided by standardized news values, producing standardized stories in standardized formats that are presented in standardized styles. The result is extraordinary sameness and minimal differentiation.

It is clear that journalists and newspapers do not want to be in the contemporary labor market, much less the highly competitive information market. They prefer to justify the value they create in the moral philosophy terms of instrumental value. Most believe that what they do is so intrinsically good and that they should be compensated to do it even if it doesn't produce revenue.

This is precisely what your organization is facing. Over time, drip by drip, year by year, the manual was written, the procedures were set, and people were hired to follow the rules. The organization gets extremely efficient at producing a certain output a certain way. Then competition or change or technology arrives, and the old rules aren't particularly useful, the old efficiencies not so profitable.

In the face of a threat like this, the natural reaction is trying to become more efficient. Run fewer pages, do some strategic layoffs (lay off the weird outliers or the expensive old-timers). The *New York Times* recently responded by making their Sunday magazine smaller and replacing the typeface with one that crams more words on each page.

Of course, this isn't the answer. Doing more of what you were doing, but more obediently, more measurably, and more averagely (is that a word?) will not solve the problem. It will make it worse. Making the resistance happy is not the same as succeeding. What do you say to your board of directors? You don't scare them with bold plans; instead, you hunker down, give in to the trend, and die slowly.

The *Politico* and the *Huffington Post*, which soon will make more money than any newspapers in the country, threw out the rules. They have no printing plants, no revered style manual, not even a fancy building. Instead, they're staffing up with artists and change makers. When they succeed, it will be because they confronted the resistance.

THIS WORKS

You'd think that the biggest self-doubt would be the potential of failure. And no doubt, many of us lie awake, filled with anxiety about big failures. Consider the argument that it's just as likely you'd hold back out of the fear of potential success.

If it works, then you have to do it. Then you have to do it again. Then you have to top it. If it works, your world changes. There are new threats and new challenges and new risks. That's world-class frightening.

Duncan Hines built an empire that ended up being worth more than a half billion dollars when his partner finally died in 1993. When Hines was building his brand, he used nothing more than some postage stamps and a printing press. He was a door-to-door salesman who wrote a restaurant guide in his spare time.

It took at least ten years for Duncan Hines the man to become Duncan Hines the world-famous brand. Any time during those ten years, a better-organized, better-capitalized competitor could have wiped him out. Your grandparents could have done it. By that time, there was no doubt that what Hines was doing was going to work. He wasn't hiding his success; it was well chronicled. No, the risk for someone challenging him was that he might compete and actually win. That would change everything.

Fast-forward fifty years, and the very same inclinations and fears are at work. Why didn't the countless smart people running newspapers around the country see what was happening online and actually organize to take advantage of it? Why is Carolyn Reidy, president and CEO of fabled book publisher Simon & Schuster, fighting against the Kindle tooth and nail?

Our society has carved out some professions where one is expected to be creative for a living. And yet, even in the movies, visual arts, and book publishing, the systems we have in place make it far easier to fake the act of creativity than to actually embrace it. The art each of us is capable of creating is relentlessly whittled away. Ask editors and agents in these industries for horror stories, and they're sure to tell you about someone who "went a little too far" and ended up getting laughed out of a job. The thing is, it's always the same story about the same guy, because examples are few and far between.

Our economy has reached a logical conclusion. The race to make average stuff for average people in huge quantities is almost over. We're hitting an asymptote, a natural ceiling for how cheaply and how fast we can deliver uninspired work.

Becoming more average, quicker, and cheaper is not as productive as it used to be.

Manufacturing a box that can play music went from $10,000 for a beautiful Edison Victrola to $2,000 for a home stereo to $300 for a Walkman to $200 for an iPod to $9 for an MP3 memory stick. Improvements in price are now so small they're hardly worth making. Now you see the reason for me asking you to be Açai Strong.

Shipping an idea went from taking a month by boat to a few days by plane to overnight by FedEx to a few minutes by fax to a moment by e-mail to instantaneous by Twitter. Now what? Will it arrive yesterday?

So what's left is to create—something remarkable. What's left is the generosity and humanity worth paying for.

PROOF OF RESISTING

It may be the resistance that's keeping you from embracing the ideas in this book. (Or it might be that I didn't make my case, but I'm betting on the former.) You're uncomfortable or skeptical or outright angry, but you're not sure why.

I mean, why not try art? How hard would it be to try?

You call the resisting "hard-hearted capitalist common sense." Perhaps you call it "being realistic about the economic forecast we are in." It's better, I think, to call it stalling, a waste, and an insidious plot to keep you from doing your real work.

BEING AFRAID OF PUBLIC SPEAKING

Why is it that a common, safe, and important task is so feared by so many people?

In *Iconoclast*, Gregory Berns, PhD, uses his experience running a neuroscience research lab to explain the biological underpinning of this mentality. In fact, public speaking is the perfect petri dish for exposing what makes us tick.

It turns out that the three biological factors driving a company's performance and innovation are social intelligence/domain knowledge, fear response, and perception. Public speaking brings all three together. Speaking to a group requires social intelligence. We need to be able to make an emotional connection with people, talk about what they are interested in, and persuade them. That's difficult, and we're not wired for this as well as we are wired to, say, eat fried foods.

Public speaking also triggers huge fear responses. Strangers or people of power, all of whom might harm us, surround us. Attention is focused on us, and attention (according to our biology) equals danger.

Last, and more subtly, speaking involves perception. It exposes how we see things, both what we are talking about and the response of the people in the room. Exposing that perception is scary.

In a contest between the rational desire to spread an idea by giving a speech and the biological phobia against it, biology has an unfair advantage.

WHERE IS THE FEAR?

If there is no sale, look for the fear.

If a marketing meeting ends in a stalemate, look for the fear.

If someone has a tantrum, breaks a promise, or won't cooperate, there's fear involved.

Fear is the most important emotion we have. It kept our ancestors alive, and may very well save our children, after all. Fear dominates the other emotions, because without our ability to avoid death, the other ones don't matter very much.

Our sanitized, corporative society hasn't figured out how to get rid of fear, so instead, we channel it into bizarre corners of our life. We check Twitter because of our fear of being left out of the loop. We buy expensive handbags for the same reason. We take a mundane follow-the-manual approach to business because of our fear of failing as a mapmaker, and we make bad financial decisions because of our fear of taking responsibility for our money.

It turns out that we're even afraid to talk about fear, as if that somehow makes it more real.

Fear of living without a map is the main reason companies are so insistent that financial projections tell them what to do.

The reasons are pretty obvious: If it's someone else's map, it's not your fault if it doesn't work out. If you've memorized the sales script I gave you, and you don't make the sale, who's in trouble now? Not only does the map insulate us from responsibility, but it's also a social talisman. We can tell our friends and family that we've found a good map, a safe map, and a map worthy of respect.

FEAR IS SELF-FULFILLING

If the meeting you're about to call is the biggest, most important do-or-die moment of your business, you're likely to feel some resistance and a lot of fear—which will not help the meeting go better. In fact, in negotiations, presentations, and other interactions, the smell of fear is the best indicator we are not to trust the other side.

THE MORE FEAR YOU HAVE, THE WORSE IT GOES

One antidote is to pursue multiple paths, generating different ways to win. This meeting or that proposal no longer means everything. If nothing is do-or-die, then you don't have to worry so much about the dying part. Confidence is self-fulfilling as well. If you can bring more of it to an interaction, you're more likely to succeed. Which, of course, creates more confidence for the next interaction. The system can bring you up, or it can bring you down. It's up to you.

Effort gets you to this nice spot; effort and planning are tools to beat the fear before it beats you.

THE PARADOX OF THE SAFETY ZONE

Fear would like you to curl up in a corner, avoid all threats, take no risks, and hide. It feels safe, after all.

The paradox is that the more you hide, the riskier it is. The less commotion you cause, the more likely you are to fail, to be ignored, and to expose yourself to failure. We tried to set up an economy where you could hide your big ideas, go through the motions, and get what you needed. That's not working so well now.

SYMPTOMS OF A SCARED COMPANY

Fear is everywhere, all the time. Its goal is to make you safe, which means invisible and unchanged. Visibility is dangerous. It leads to the possibility of people laughing at you, or even death. Change is dangerous because it involves moving from the known to the unknown, and that might be dangerous.

So fear is wily. It works to do one of two things: get you to fit in (and become invisible) or get you to fail (which makes it unlikely that positive change will arrive, thus permitting you to stay still).

Here are some signs that fear is at work:

- Don't ship on time. Late is the first step to never.

- Procrastinate, claiming that you need to be perfect.

- Ship early, sending out defective ideas, hoping they will be rejected.
- Suffer anxiety about what product to bring to the next convention.
- Make excuses involving lack of money.
- Do excessive networking, with the goal of having everyone like you and support you.
- Engage in deliberately provocative behavior designed to ostracize you so you'll have no standing in the community.
- Demonstrate a lack of desire to obtain new skills.
- Spend hours on obsessive data collection. (Jeffrey Eisenberg reports, "79 percent of businesses obsessively capture Internet traffic data, yet only 30 percent of them changed their sites as a result of analysis.")
- Be snarky.
- Start committees instead of taking action.
- Join committees instead of leading.
- Excessively criticize the work of your competitors, thus unrealistically raising the bar for your work.
- Produce deliberately outlandish work and products that no one can possibly embrace.
- Ship deliberately average work, products that will certainly fit in and be ignored.
- Don't ask questions.
- Ask too many questions.
- Criticize anyone who is doing something differently. If they succeed, that means you'll have to do something different, too.
- Start a never-ending search for the next big thing, abandoning yesterday's great thing as old.
- Embrace an emotional attachment to the status quo.
- Invent anxiety about the side effects of a new approach.

- Be boring.
- Focus on revenge or teaching someone a lesson, at the expense of doing the work.
- Slow down as the deadline for completion approaches. Check your work obsessively as ship the date looms.
- Wait for tomorrow.
- Manufacture anxiety about people stealing your ideas.
- When you find behaviors that increase the chances of shipping, stop using them.
- Believe it's about the gifts and talents, not skill.
- Announce you have neither.

This list is unusual in that I'm highlighting the up and the down, the left and the right. Any direction you go instead of the direction that succeeds is the work of fear.

It's interesting to say it out loud: "I'm not performing to my potential because of my fear."

When you say it out loud (not think about it, but say it), the fear retreats in shame.

"I DON'T KNOW WHAT TO DO" AND OTHER CLASSIC QUOTES FROM FEAR

"I don't have any good ideas."

Actually, you don't have any bad ideas. If you get enough bad ideas, the good ones will take care of themselves. And as every successful company will tell you, the ideas aren't the hard part. It's shipping that's difficult.

"I don't know what to do."

This one is certainly true. The question is, why does that bother you? No one actually knows what to do. Sometimes we have a hunch or a good idea, but we're never sure. The art of challenging the resistance is doing something when you're not certain it's going to work.

"I didn't graduate from [insert brand of some prestigious educational institution here]."

Well, MIT is now free online, for anyone who wants to learn. The public library in your town has just about everything you need, and what's not there is online. Access to knowledge used to matter. No longer.

"Well, that's fine for you, but my gender, race, health, religion, nationality, shoe size, handicap, or DNA don't make it easy."

Can't you just hear the fear behind every word in this question? Precisely how many counterexamples do you need before you get over this excuse?

THE PRODUCT

Your real work, then, what you might be paid for and what is certainly your passion, is simple: the product.

Your work is to create things, to expose your insight and humanity in such a way that you are truly indispensable.

Your work is to do the work, not to do your job. Your job is about following instructions; the work is about making a difference. Your work is to ship. Ship things that make change.

BUILT TO SHIP

The habit that successful companies have developed is simple: they thrash a lot at the start, because starting means they are going to finish—not maybe, not probably, but going to.

If you want to produce things on time and on budget, all you have to do is work until you run out of time or run out of money, then ship.

No room for stalling or excuses or the resistance. On ship date, it's gone.

IS IT IMPORTANT ENOUGH?

There's only one "you," only one driver's license per company. You're going to invent what you're going to invent, do what you're going to do.

Van Gogh wasn't wired to paint. Paint was the medium available to him at the time. If he had lived today, perhaps he would have marketed organic tofu. It's not predetermined that you'll hold a paintbrush or write a symphony. It is predetermined, however, that you have the ability to succeed with effort.

That means you have to choose your art. It's not preordained; there isn't only one art for you.

If you pick something that is not challenging to you, then the resistance will win. After all, what's the point of overcoming the pain the bad products inflict if all you're doing is something that doesn't matter much anyway? Overcoming excuses and social challenges isn't easy, and it won't happen if the end result isn't worth it. Trivial art isn't worth the trouble it takes to produce it.

When you set down the path to create your products, whatever sort of art it is, understand that the path is neither short nor easy. That means you must determine if the route is worth the effort. If it's not, dream bigger.

The temptation to sabotage the new thing is huge, precisely because the new thing might work.

THE INTERNET IS CRACK COCAINE FOR THE RESISTANCE

If your employees sit around at work all day watching *Price Is Right* reruns, you will probably be going out of business soon. But it's apparently fine to tweak and update your company's Facebook account for an hour. That's "connecting to your social graph."

There's a big part of our psyche that wants to touch and be touched. We want to be connected, valued, and missed. We want people to know we exist, and we don't want to get bored.

Don't even get me started on Twitter. There are certainly people who are using it effectively and productively. Some people (a few) are finding that it helps them do the work. But the rest? It's perfect resistance, because it's never done. There's always another tweet to be read and responded to. Which, of course, keeps you from doing the work.

Where did your art go while you were tweeting?

WHERE DO YOU HIDE BRILLIANCE?

Where do you hide your insight? You have plenty of big ideas, no shortage of breakthroughs. A friend of mine (an entrepreneur) says something really smart every day, something earth shattering once a week. And that's it. At the end of the year, he has some great blog posts and a pile of tweets to show for it. What if he harnessed even one of those ideas and fought the resistance hard enough to actually make something of it?

At the end of the year, he could show us a multi-dollar company or a movement that changed the world. By the end of the year, he could have leveraged a few of those ideas into a promotion, a corner office, and a parking space. The only difference between my friend and companies that change everything is the resistance.

TICK, TICK, TICK
This is my first book.

When I started my career, I was a marketing associate. My team and I created more than a hundred campaigns, working with various companies. After that, I started and sold an Internet company (now bankrupt because of poor leadership), then started another job (which I hated), gave some speeches, and started another Internet company.

Am I some sort of prodigy? I don't think so. I ship. I don't get in the way of the muse, I fight the resistance, and I ship. I do this by not doing an enormous number of tasks that are perfect stalling devices, ideal ways of introducing the resistance into our lives.

A workaholic brings fear into the equation. She works all the time to be sure everything is all right, and she experiences resistance all the time.

I'm not a workaholic. There's no fear because I've ingrained the habit of shipping.

By forcing myself to do absolutely no busywork tasks in between bouts of work, I remove the best excuse of the resistance. I can't avoid the work because I am not distracting myself with anything but the work. This is the hallmark of a productive artist. I don't go to meetings. I don't write memos. I don't have a staff. I don't commute. The goal is to strip away anything that looks productive but doesn't involve shipping.

It takes crazy discipline to do nothing between projects. It means you have to face a blank wall and you can't look bust. It means you are alone with your thoughts, and it means a new project, perhaps a great project, will appear pretty soon, because your restless energy can't permit you to only sit and do nothing.

Leo Babauta's brilliant little book *Zen Habits* helps you think your way through this problem. His program is simple: attempt to create only one significant work a year. Break that into smaller projects, and every day, find three tasks to accomplish that will help you complete a project. And do only those tasks during your work hours. I'm talking about an hour a day to complete a mammoth work of art, whatever sort of art you have in mind. That hour a day might not be fun, but it's probably a lot more productive than the ten hours you spend now.

Companies sabotage Leo's idea every day. They try to do the significant project, and at the same time, they pay lip service (and devote time) to all that surface nonsense that critics say you're supposed to spend your time on. Since they try to do both, they accomplish neither. Or they pretend their project is significant, but it's actually trivial and far below them.

The difference between a successful businesses and a failed one happens after the idea is hatched. The difference is the race to completion. Did you finish?

SPRINT!

The best way to overcome your fear of creativity, brainstorming, intelligent risk-taking, or navigating a tricky situation might be to sprint.

When we sprint, all the internal dialogue falls away, and we focus on going as fast as we possibly can. When you're sprinting, you don't feel that sore knee, and you don't worry that the ground isn't perfectly level. You just run.

You can't sprint forever. That's what makes it sprinting. The brevity of the event is a key part of why it works.

"Quick, you have thirty minutes to come up with the business ideas."

"Hurry, we need to write a new script for our commercial—we have fifteen minutes."

My first huge project after college was launching a major brand of science adventure games. I stopped going to graduate school classes in order to do the launch.

One day, right after a red-eye flight, the president of the company didn't have enough resources to launch all the products we had planned, our progress was too slow, and the packaging wasn't ready yet.

I went to my office and spent the next twenty hours rewriting every word of text, redesigning every package, rebuilding every schedule, and inventing a new promotional strategy. It was probably six weeks of work for a motivated committee, and I did it (alone) in one fell swoop. Like lifting a car off a baby, it was impossible, and I have absolutely no recollection of the project now.

The board saw the finished work, reconsidered, and the project was back on again. I didn't get scared until after the sprint—then I passed out. You can't sprint every day, but it's probably a good idea to sprint regularly. It keeps the resistance at bay.

DOWNHILL VERSUS UPHILL

Launching your company into the world often feels like an uphill climb, an ongoing series of challenges and obstacles. At any step along the way, the resistance can cut you down. All you need to do is falter, and your work is wasted. You're pushing a rock uphill, and if you stop for a second, the thing rolls all the way down, erasing all your effort.

It's possible, though, to view the work that comes with the launching of your products as an inevitable gravitational process, like an avalanche or a giant slalom. Start at the top of the hill, not the bottom. One little step to get you started, and then it grows, ever faster. No amount of resistance can stop this from happening.

The Internet can amplify this effect. You put up a video, and then in a week, a million people have seen it. You send an e-mail message to the right six people, and a project begins.

That's why authors enjoy having book publishers. Even though it's technically easy to publish your own book, technically easy to get it typeset or printed or even put into a bookstore, authors with a choice rarely self-publish. That's because the current system is such a powerful amplifier. Send your manuscript to your agent. He or she sells it to a publisher (no pushing necessary on your behalf). The publisher does all the difficult tasks of bringing your work to the market, tasks that your brain would gladly sabotage.

If there's an infrastructure (like a publisher) in place to amplify your insights, that's great. Often, though, it's not there. The firms that take that money to patent your idea and promote it, for example, or the fraudulent contests that charge you money to enter a competition to win a prize—these prey on people who haven't built a platform. You need a platform that makes it easy to turn your insight into a movement.

I'm trying to sell you on the idea of building a platform before you have your next idea, to view the platform building as a separate project from spreading your art. You can work on the platform every day; do it without facing the resistance. As the platform gets bigger and stronger, you get to launch each idea a little farther uphill.

It's not easy to get to this point. A valuable platform is an asset, one that isn't handed to you. It takes preparation and effort to set up the work so that your ideas are more likely to ship. But that's effort that the resistance won't be so eager to sabotage. By separating the hard work of preparation from the scary work of insight, you can build an environment in which you're more likely to ship.

ONE WAY TO THRASH AND OVERCOME RESISTANCE

Here's how I make stuff.

I've used this technique to launch projects, write my book, plan vacations, work in teams, work solo, and write a blog—all projects that ship on time.

The first step is to write down the due date. Post it on the wall. You will ship on this date, done or not.

The next step is to use index cards, Post-it notes, Moleskine notebooks, fortune cookies—whatever you can embrace. Write down every single notion, plan, idea, sketch, and contact. This is when you go fishing. Get as much help as you like. Invite as many people as you can. This is their big chance.

This is where the thrashing and dreaming begin. It's very hard to get the people you work with to pay attention at this moment. Since the deadline is so far away, their brains are asleep, and there's no fear or selfish motivation available. People focus on emergencies, not urgencies, and getting yourself (and them) to stop working tomorrow's deadline and pitch in now isn't easy. A big part of the work, then, is to get yourself (and your team, if you have one) to step up and dream.

On a regular basis, collect the cards and read them aloud to the team. This process will inevitably lead to more cards.

Then put the cards into a database. I use FileMaker Pro, but you can use any simple database. (You can even use a pad of paper.) If you have a group, try to find a group database for the Web. Every card gets its own record.

The record can include words, images, sketches, and links to other cards. The idea is that this is your thrashing playground. Let the team play along. Rearrange. Draw. Sketch. Make sure everyone understands that this is the very last chance he or she has to make the project better.

One person (that would be you) then goes through the database and builds a complete description of the project. If it's a book, then you've got a forty-page outline. If it's a website, then you have every single screen and feature. If it's a conference, then you have an agenda, a menu, a list of venues, and so on. It's the blueprint.

Take this blueprint NOT to everyone but to the few people who have sign-off control, the people with money. They can approve it, cancel the project, or suggest a few compromises.

Then say, "If I deliver what you approved, on budget and on time, will you ship it?"

Don't proceed until you get a yes. Iterate if you must, but don't get started simply because you're in a hurry. Do not accept "Well, I'll know it when I see it." Not allowed.

Once you get your yes, go away and build your project, thrash-free. Ship on time, because that's what the Açai Strong does.

RETHINKING YOUR GOALS IN LIGHT OF THE FEAR

What does the success of your project look like? Have you defined success in terms of critics, or some other measure that doesn't actually serve your needs? Are you hoping for a great review or a gold star or applause? A profit? Big sales? Changing people's minds? The chance to do it again?

The resistance is happy to set up unachievable goals as a way of dissuading you from doing the work. After all, if it's important to achieve something and it's going to be painful to try, why bother? When we agree to define our success on others' terms, especially other people who don't particularly like us and aren't inclined to root for us, we're giving in to the resistance.

If you do decide you want to please the critics, the same people who make a living hating the sort of thing you do, it's easy to give up in advance.

If you declare that you want to build a giant brand, something in the top fifty brands of all time, it's easy to hit roadblocks. That's because your goal is largely impossible. The roadblocks don't make your project more likely to succeed; they kill it.

The Grateful Dead puzzled industry pundits for a long time. Why didn't they want to sell more records? Why didn't they want a gold record? Why didn't they want to get their music played on the radio? The answer is simple: they were playing a different game, a different tune. Instead of buying into the system that would tear them down and corrupt their vision, they built their own system, one that was largely resistance-proof. One concert a night, night after night, for decade after decade.

Play only for people you like, with people you enjoy.

The result is sneaky and effective. When you haven't set up a judge and jury for your work, you get to do art that doesn't alert the resistance. And then you can leverage that art into the next thing.

AMPLIFYING THOUGHTS

Do you remember what you had for lunch yesterday? If you take a second, you probably do. Now, do you remember what internal dialogue and little thoughts you had racing through your mind a few minutes before lunch yesterday? Almost certainly not.

Little thoughts are ephemeral. They come, and inevitably, they go. We don't remember them an hour later, never mind a week or a month later.

A few years ago, I came up with the idea for "Disposable Marketing." In the shower. I still remember the where and the when. It was one of those little ideas, something that could easily disappear. The resistance would be happy if all your little brainstorms disappeared, because then they wouldn't represent a threat, would they?

The challenge is in being alert enough to write them down, to prioritize them, to build them, and to ship them out the door. It's a habit, it's easy to learn, and it's frightening.

THE RESISTANCE GETS ITS NEXT EXCUSE READY IN ADVANCE

Are you in the wrong industry? Does your spouse hold you back? Is it the economy? Perhaps it's the vendetta your competitors have always had against you.

The resistance is working overtime to be sure that you won't actually do anything remarkable. As a result, the list of excuses in reserve is longer than you might expect. When it finds a useful crutch, a loser's limp, the resistance will milk it for all it's worth. But removing that excuse, calling the bluff, probably won't be sufficient. There's always another one at the ready.

The only solution is to call all the bluffs at once, to tolerate no rational or irrational reason to hold back on your art. The only solution is to start today, to start now, and to ship at the end.

9

❖ ❖ ❖

açai strong
and powerful

GIFTS?

I must have been absent that day at Harvard Business School.

They don't spend a lot of time teaching you about the power of unreciprocated gifts, about the long (fifty thousand years) tradition of tribal economies built around the idea of mutual support and generosity. In fact, I don't think the concept is even mentioned once. We've been so brainwashed it doesn't even occur to us that there might be an alternative to "How much should I charge? How much can I make?"

There are three reasons why it's now urgent to understand how the gifts culture works. First, the Internet (and digital goods) has lowered the marginal cost of generosity. Second, it's impossible for your company to be açai without understanding the power that giving a gift creates. And third, the dynamic of gift giving can diminish the cries of the resistance and permit you to do your best work.

The very fact that gift giving without recompense feels uncomfortable is reason enough for you to take a moment to find out why.

GIVING, RECEIVING, GIVING

In the beginning, there was the culture of gifts. Caveman culture has a long tradition of reciprocity, and as Marcel Mauss has written, this reciprocity was used to build relationships and power. In the Pacific Northwest, Native American tribal leaders established their power by giving everything away. They could afford to give everyone a gift, because they were so powerful and the gifts were a symbol of that power. Any leader who hoarded saw his power quickly diminish. Mauss argues that there is no such thing as a free gift. Everyone who gives a gift, he asserts, wants something in return.

Then, quite suddenly, this ancient tradition changed. Money and structured society flipped the system, and now you get and don't give. Author Lewis Hyde reminds us that, for the last few centuries, our society views the winner as the person who receives the most gifts. To receive a gift makes you a king, a rich person, someone worth currying favor with. It feels totally appropriate that people in power are pandered to. It turns out, though, that this is a fairly recent behavior. Power used to be about giving, not getting. The powerful companies should do more than receive the consumers' money.

In the açai economy, the winners are once again the companies that give gifts. Giving a gift makes you indispensable. Inventing a gift, creating art—that is what the market seeks out, and the givers are the ones who earn our respect and attention and dollars. Shephard Fairey didn't seek to monetize the Obama Hope poster. He gave it away with a single-minded obsession. The more copies he gave away, the closer he came to achieving his political, personal, and professional goals.

Part of the reason for this flip is the digital nature of our new gift system. If I create an idea, the Internet makes it possible for that gift to spread everywhere, quite quickly, at no cost to my company or me. Digital gifts, ideas that spread—these allow the genius companies to be far more generous than they ever could have been in an analog world.

Thomas Hawk is the most successful digital photographer in the world. He has taken tens of thousands of pictures on his way to his goal of taking a million in his lifetime. The remarkable thing about Hawk's rise is that his pictures are licensed under the Creative Commons License and are freely shared with anyone, with no permission required for personal use. Thomas is both an artist and a giver of gifts. As a result, he leads a movement, he has plenty of paid work, and he is known for his talents. In short, he is indispensable.

When users of the online review site Yelp ganged up on a pizzeria in San Francisco, management didn't sue. Instead, they got creative and gave generously. Pizzeria Delfina outfitted its servers with T-shirts emblazoned with the most ridiculous one-star criticisms the place had received. The idea spread, and the T-shirts have shown up online around the world. They cost next to nothing, but they make millions of people smile. Delfina gave a gift to its loyal customers by making fun of itself.

THERE ARE NO GENIUSES ON THE ASSEMBLY LINE

As soon as it's part of a system, it's no longer art. Artistic companies shake things up. They invent as they go; they respond to inputs and create surprising new outputs. That's why MBAs often have trouble pigeonholing in these types of companies. The artistic can't be easily instructed, predicted, or measured, and that's precisely what you are taught to do in business school.

Consumers love artists. So do investors. That's because art represents a chance to improve the status quo, not just make it cheaper. Art builds a community, and the community creates value for all.

When U2 goes on tour, the tour is an opportunity to do new art every night. The moment the band turns the tour into a cookie-cutter system to earn money, it ceases to be art and becomes a souvenir factory.

There are services online that will take your photograph and turn it into an Andy Warhol–style silk screen. While this might be creative, it's not art. Any time you can say, "this style," it has ceased to be art and started to be a process.

SELFISH

Robert Ringer wrote *Looking Out for Number One,* one of the most damaging business books I've ever read. His salute to selfishness was a product of its time, and it rubbed a lot of people the wrong way.

Becoming an açai company is not an act of selfishness. I see it as an act of generosity, because it gives you a platform for expending emotional labor and giving gifts. There are plenty of companies that fear the idea of indispensable competitors and would instead encourage you to focus on trends. "Trends" is the word critics and MBAs and professors use when they actually mean, "Do what I say." It's not trendy to stand by and do whatever the market or the critics tells you to. It might be cooperative or complaint or useful, but it's not trendsetting.

The only way I know of to become a successful business is to build a support team of fellow geniuses. The goal is to have an impact, and while it starts with the company (this is my gift, my effort), it works only when it is gratefully accepted by your team and your customers.

THE CURSE OF GIVING IT BACK

It's human nature. If someone gives you a gift, you need to reciprocate.

If someone invites you over for dinner, you bring wine. If people give you a Christmas gift, you can't rest until you give them one back.

It's reciprocity that turned the gift system into the gift economy. Suddenly, giving a gift becomes an obligation, one demanding payment, not a gift at all. So marketers use the reciprocity impulse against consumers, using gifts as a come-on. "Buy one get one free," it's everywhere.

This can cripple art.

A server does his art for table twelve regardless of whether or not those customers are big tippers. An artist paints his painting without knowing if someone is going to buy it.

The magic of the gift system is that the gift is voluntary, not part of a contract. The gift binds the recipient to the giver, and both of them to the community. A contract isolates individuals, with money as the connector. The gift binds them instead.

GIFTS AS A SIGNAL OF SURPLUS

It's difficult to be generous when you're hungry because you need to raise revenue.

Yet being generous keeps you from going hungry, hence the conflict.

A business coach writes and gives away a two-hundred-page e-book jammed with useful tips and secrets. Everything he knows, online, for free. Is this generous or stupid? Is there an easier way to make it clear that he has wisdom to spare?

Gifts not only satisfy our needs as artistic companies, but they also signal to the world that we have plenty more to share. This perspective is magnetic. The more you have in your cup, the more likely people are to want a drink. If I meet you at a party, I hope you'll ask me for free marketing/business advice. I'm always amazed that people are willing to listen to what I have to say, and I'm happy to share. The act of giving the gift is worth more to me than it may be to you to receive it.

MARTIN LUTHER AND THE BEGINNING OF THE MONEY CULTURE

The Protestant Reformation permitted the explosion of commerce that led to the world we live in now. Once the Reformation began to spread, powerful local interests heavily lobbied Martin Luther. In response, he gave princes and landlords the moral authority to take over the commons and rent the land back to the people who lived on it.

The new church was looking for political support, and its embrace of mercantilism guaranteed that it would get that support from power brokers that had chafed under the Catholic Church's opposition to the practice of charging interest and the commercialization of formerly common lands. (The Catholic Church wanted to keep local lords, princes, and kings weak, of course, because it was built around a strong universal leader, the pope.)

One of the factors in the growth of the Protestant Reformation was the commercial interest that supported its spread because of the need for a moral authority to lend and borrow money. It's hard to overestimate how large of a shift this led to in the world's culture and economics.

As Thomas Jefferson wrote, it created a world where "the merchant has no homeland." If everyone is a stranger, it's a lot easier to do business. If everyone is a stranger, then we can charge for things that used to be gifts. The merchant class was essential to imperialism and to the growth of the money culture, but it can't exist without a culture that encourages money lending.

This thinking destroyed many traditional societies but permitted the growth of commerce-based organizations. The East India Company or the fashion houses of France or the banks of Italy never could have existed in a world that honored a ban on usury.

Martin Luther saw that embracing the needs of local power brokers could enhance the spread of Protestantism. With little alternative, the pope followed suit. The ban on usury was refined, double-talked, and eventually, eliminated. The money flowed, investments were made, businesses grew, and productivity soared. People could view every transaction as a chance to lend or make money because they were independent agents. Everyone became a businessperson, a borrower, or a lender.

Suddenly, your community was a profit center. If you knew a lot of people, you could make money from them. Social leadership magically translated into financial leadership.

10

❖ ❖ ❖

gift giving in practice

For five hundred years, since the legalization of usury and the institutionalization of money, almost every element of our lives has been about commerce.

If you did something or produced something, you did it for the money, or because it would lead to money. Sure, you still don't charge your kids for dinner, but you also don't encourage your kids to sweep up at the mall for free. Why should they? It's someone's job.

Example: I'm going downtown by cab from the Regan National Airport. There are forty fellow travelers in the cab line. If I call out, "Anyone want to share a cab to the Marriott?" People look at me funny. They don't want to owe me for the ride, don't want to interact, and don't want to open themselves up to the connection that will occur from taking my gift of a ride. They'd rather pay for it, clean and square, and stay isolated. It's hard to imagine two Bedouin tribespeople isolating from each other with such enthusiasm.

Gifts have been relegated to cash substitutes. If I give you a gift, the only apparent reason is to get you to reciprocate. It's like giving you cash, but with social cover. The studio chief may think, "I can give Seth Rogan a pinball machine for Christmas, because then he'll owe me and the next negotiation might go better."

The first problem, of course, with these sorts of gifts is that they ruin true gifts, while the second problem is that they are poor cash substitutes. They create misunderstandings and confusion because if Seth Rogen doesn't value the pinball machine the way the studio head does, one side or the other is going to be upset.

Real gifts don't demand reciprocation (at least not direct reciprocation in cash), and the best kinds of gifts are art and connection.

NARCOTICS ANONYMOUS AND GIFTS

A critical underpinning at NA is that no money changes hands. There's no central organization collecting dues, no fee to attend a meeting, no payments from one member to another. The act of helping a fellow addict for free has two effects: first, it brings the giver and the recipient closer together, creating a society, and second, it creates an obligation for the recipient. Not an obligation to reciprocate, because she really can't and it's not expected, but an obligation to help the next person.

And so the movement grows.

THE DIFFERENCE BETWEEN DEBT AND EQUITY

When someone invests in your business and takes some founder's stock, he gets closer to you. He is on your side, because when you win, he wins.

When a bank loans you money for college, it becomes the other. The bank is opposed to you, sapping your resources and taking money first, not last. College loans are the ones you can't discharge, even in bankruptcy. The bank that made the loan usually sells it, so there's no connection to you any longer. The bank doesn't offer counseling or peer support or even to check in with you about your career choices. They just demand to be paid. No equity investor would act this way. (Message to banks: please be more social.)

There are many forms of equity, and a few of them involve cash. When you invest time or resources into someone's success or happiness, and your payment is a share of that outcome, you become partners. Our consumers are silent partners with equity in our companies.

WHAT DOES ALL THIS HAVE TO DO WITH YOU?

Are you giving gifts? Really and truly? Or are you so beaten down by the system, so indoctrinated by it, that you can't imagine creating art and getting closer to the consumers who matter to you?

If this section on gifts and debts and reciprocity feels strange, it's a symptom of how much humanity has been drummed out of you by a commercial imperative run amok, or possibly, it's a symptom that you've forgotten that you even have the ability to give these gifts. The system can make you feel taken advantage of, abused, exploited by the "commercial imperative." You're just a player in the commercial machine. Realizing you haven't given gifts because you're scared or that you've forgotten what you have to offer might compel you to action.

I think it's worth a try.

THE CIRCLES OF THE GIFT MODULE

While some artists get rich (J.K. Rowling got very rich), making art is not about getting rich. Art is a gift, a gift from the artist to the viewer, the listener, and the user. The moment it ceases to be a gift, some of the art is lost.

However, a change has happened to the working life of a typical artist. Now, your art can reach much further and affect more people than ever before. An indie singer can reach a million people with her gift, not just a crowded coffeehouse. An industrial designer can impact the lives of a billion people with a new way to filter water.

Many businesses have fretted about the economics of this cost-free spread of art in all its forms, but the real magic is the leverage this expansion adds, not the loss of commerce it causes. When you have more friends in the core circle, more people with whom to share your art, your products are amplified and can have more power and even bigger revenue.

Remember, we're most likely to give gifts to our family and friends. We don't charge them interest, and they are not customers; they are people we embrace.

The Internet is changing the circle we call "friends and family." Twitter and Facebook created a new class of people; call them "friendlikes." If I can give the gift of art, for free, to my expanding circle of friendlikes, why would I hesitate?

Three circles have traditionally defined the cycle of art among fine artists, such as painters and sculptors.

I think these circles can work for anyone giving a gift or making a change in the world.

The first circle represents true gifts—items that an artist gleefully and willingly shares. This circle is comprised of employees, friends, or family, or the people with whom you work. If someone comes over for dinner, you don't charge him or her. The meal is a gift. If friends ask for a stock tip or accounting help, you don't charge them. It's a gift.

The second circle is the circle of commerce. In this circle are people who pay organizations for art. They pay for a souvenir edition or a poster or a speech. They pay for consulting or a house concert or a newsletter subscription.

And now, the Internet creates a third circle, the circle of your society, your followers, fans who may become friendlikes. It's huge and it's important, because it enables you to affect more people and improve more lives.

Monet gave paintings to friends (the first circle) or sold them to collectors (the second circle).

These, in turn, were sold for very high prices, sometimes after his death. The paintings were resold to people who needed to possess them, or who wanted to resell them, or to one way control them.

Those paintings hang in museums, where they can be seen for free (or a small donation) by the masses (the third circle).

This third circle changes art for all artists, forever. It means that you can share your gift with more people, cheaper and quicker than ever before. When you focus on the second circle, your art suffers. Instead, we profit most when we make the first and third circles as big as we can. Generosity generates income. This works whether you are selling paintings or innovation or a service.

Linus Torvalds worked hard to create the Linux operating system. He did it for free, and he did it largely for his friends. The Internet permitted him to jump to a third circle, a hundred million or more people around the world who benefit from his art, who participate in his community and follow his work.

As the third circle grows in size, the second circle takes care of itself. Linus and the core team responsible for Linux will never need to look for work again, because as you give more and more to the friendlikes, the list of people willing to pay you to do your work always grows.

THE DIFFERENCE BETWEEN "IF" AND "AND"

In a monetary exchange, we focus on "if." I will give you this *if* you give me that. The initial exchange depends on the promise of reciprocity and doesn't occur without it. In a gift, we imply "and." I will give you this, *and* you will do something for someone else. I will give you this, *and* my expectation is that it will change the way you feel.

The power lies in the creation of abundance. A trade leaves things as they were, with no external surplus. A gift always creates a surplus as it spreads. And it encourages consumers to return, this time even more willing to pay for our products.

WASHING RENTAL CARS

My friend Camille used to say, "No one washes a rental car before they return it." The reason should now be obvious: Avis is not a member of our circle. I paid for the car, and they got the money, so they should wash it. It's a transaction.

Transactions distance parties from one another. The transaction establishes the rules of engagement, and if it's not in the rules, you don't have to worry about it. If I eat in your restaurant tonight and pay my check, there's no obligation for me to return tomorrow or for you to send me a Christmas card. We had a deal, a deal's a deal (what a great expression), and we can move on. In many ways, this anti-connection relationship brings a great deal of freedom to our commerce and allows things to grow and spread and change quite rapidly.

Consider the alternative: the bellboy who refuses a tip for helping an elderly customer, the doctor who drives out of her way to check on a patient even though it's her day off, the restaurant owner who sends out a few special dishes to a regular customer and refuses to charge for them.

In each case, the lack of a transaction created a bond between the giver and the recipient, and perhaps surprisingly, the giver usually comes out even further ahead.

Hyatt Hotels Corporation is now treating customers differently. Since they know who their best customers are, they're working not to charge them more but to give them more. They're setting out to randomly cover bar tabs, offer free massages, and provide other services they could otherwise charge for. If they do it in a corporate, by-the-book way, it'll feel fake and will fail. But if they empower their employees to actually be generous, it can't help but work.

As we've seen, if there is no gift, there is no art. When art is created solely to be sold, it's only a commodity. A key element for the artist is the act of giving the art to someone in the circle. (To be clear, an object or a canvas or a deliverable is not necessary for it to be art. Seeing the thing, hearing the thing, understanding the thing—that's enough for it to be art.)

If I give you a piece of art, then you can't and shouldn't be busy assigning a monetary value to it. To do so is to take away its magic. If flight attendants charged extra for smiles, or helping you with a bag or entertaining your kid, that wouldn't be a gift and it wouldn't be art. It would be emotional labor for hire.

If I give you a piece of art, you shouldn't be required to work hard to reciprocate because reciprocation is an act of keeping score, which involves monetizing the art, not appreciating it. When I come to your house for dinner, I shouldn't bring brownies merely because you asked me over to dinner. To do so devalues and disrespects your gift.

An acquaintance of mine always gives a cash gift when he attends weddings, bar mitzvahs, graduations, and birthdays. He makes out the check over dessert, after the ceremony—and the amount of the check is directly related to the amount he thinks was spent on the catering. A steak dinner earns you a bigger wedding check. Sigh.

Or consider the family that exchanges cash at Christmas. If everyone is giving and getting the same amount, there's not much happening, is there?

The gift of art instantly creates a bond between the artist and the recipient. A priceless gift has been given, one that can never be valued or monetarily paid for or reciprocated. The benefit to the artist is the knowledge that you changed in some way, not that you will repay him or her. And so your only possible response is to make the circle stronger.

When companies treat you with respect or spend the time to try to change your mind, they are embracing you in the best way they can. If they touch you in any way, you then have two obligations: to make them closer and

110

to pass on their message. Gifts don't demand immediate payment, but they have always included social demands within the market. Companies that give are given the reward of publicity from their consumers.

THE SELFISH BY-PRODUCT

Some companies are gift givers by nature. They love their market or they respect their art, and so they give. Not for an ulterior motive, but because it gives them joy.

Other companies might need to consider the economic benefits first. These are companies that were brainwashed by the last five hundred years of history, companies that want to know what's in it for them; companies believe "there is no such thing as a free lunch" and "every man for himself." These are companies that have no art in their life because they're unable to give a true gift. They want something in return. They want security or cash, or both.

The hardheaded, selfish capitalists among us will enjoy the next sentence:

"Açai companies are indispensable and Açai Strong."

Art is scarce; scarcity creates value. Gifts make economies stronger. Certain organizations will strive to replace replaceable elements with cheaper substitutes. But generous companies aren't easily replaceable.

So açai companies are different.

If your business gives a gift, I hope you will do it because you respect your muse and embrace your art. But—right now, anyway—I'll settle for you simulating this behavior simply because you want to be Açai Strong, the center of the circle, the source of our inspiration, and the one we all count on to make a difference.

111

Some companies think that you can't be generous until after you become a success. They argue that they have to get theirs, and then they can go ahead and give back. The astonishing fact is that the most successful companies in the world are those who don't do it for the money.

Old-school businesspeople argue for copyright and patent protection and say, "I can't tell you my idea because I'm afraid you will steal it." Old-school thinking is that you get paid first, you sign a contract, and you protect and defend with profit. They say, "Pay me."

Açai companies say, "Here."

TWO WAYS CONSUMERS THINK ABOUT GIFTS

1. Give me a gift!
2. Here's a gift (money for your product), I love you.

The first is a capitalist misunderstanding of what it means to give or receive a gift. The second is the only valid alternative on the list.

THE MAGIC OF OPERATING BELOW YOUR MEANS

One of the reasons companies go for not giving gifts is that they can't afford it. Gifts don't have to cost money, but they always cost time and effort. If you're in a panic about money, those two things are hard to find. The reason these companies believe they can't afford it, though, is that they've bought into a consumer culture that they're in debt or have monthly bills. That makes no sense at all.

When you cut your expenses to the bone, you have a surplus. The surplus allows you to be generous, which mysteriously turns around and makes your surplus even bigger.

HOW TO RECEIVE GIFTS

It's possible to destroy a company by refusing their gifts. It's possible to destroy a company by wasting their gifts as well, or by receiving them in the wrong way.

Hollywood kills artists every day. They find an independent filmmaker who has made a wonderful gift of a film. Then they buy him off, give him too much money and not enough freedom, and choke him to death. The record industry destroys artists regularly by forcing them to conform in exchange for the promise that they will spread the gift of their art.

Why, precisely, is that customer service rep going the extra mile? What's in it for her to deliver a gift so precious when she's not in line for extra cash? Cash-focused, short-term profit seekers can't bear this. They don't want a relationship that isn't based on money, and they want to be able to turn the art on or off at will.

For some companies, the benefits are all internal. Creating art is an intrinsic good, something they enjoy. They don't want anything, don't seek anything, and if they're particularly resolute, won't get anything.

Most açai companies, though, are seeking some sort of feedback. They want to know that the art they are creating is causing a change—that it's working.

And some artists want fame and fortune.

Every company I've ever met wants to build bonds, wants to cause connections to be made. Do you think that Mark Zuckerberg wants fans stalking him, wants to be treated awkwardly wherever he goes, wants to be invited to your kid's birthday party because you know a friend of a friend of his son's? Mark doesn't want to be our friend; he wants to cause you to change or connect.

Do you think the innovative kid in the mailroom wants a fifty-dollar check in his pay envelope as payment for the new system he pushed that saves the company a million dollars a year? Is that why he did it?

A gift well received can lead to more gifts. But artists don't give gifts for money. They do it for respect and connection and to cause change. So the best recipients are the ones who can reciprocate in kind. With honest gratitude. With clear reports about the change that was created. With gifts that actually cost us, not just tiny gratuity or faux appreciation.

MANIPULATION OF THE GIFT ECONOMY

As soon as you draw the map and monetize emotional labor, you ruin it.

The pasted-on smiles of a guide at Disney World, for example, have far less power than the genuine connection a tourist makes—even for an instant—with a blue-collar worker manning the controls of the ride.

That's why telemarketers who read scripts never achieve the results of salespeople who actually speak what they believe. Big businesses have realized that people crave connection, not stuff; they've tried to institutionalize it, measure it, and reward it, and they have failed every time.

Think of the flight attendant standing at the exit to the plane, saying, "B'bye, b'bye," over and over again, doing it because she must, not because she wants to.

The intent of the giver and the posture of the recipient are critical. I'm not arguing that you must fake your attitude and cop a new behavior in order to get ahead.

Working the first-class cabin at Air France can be a nightmare job. Flight attendants wait on spoiled, tired executives for hours on end, rarely earning the service they demand. Sure, they get paid for it, but all too often, they're not open or receptive to it.

The secret of working this flight, as the people who do the work have told me, is to realize that the extraordinary service being delivered is not for the passenger and not for Air France. It's for the flight attendant. Hire people who want to make a connection with your consumers.

The most successful givers aren't doing it because they're being told to. They do it because doing it is fun. It gives them joy.

Sure, it would be better if they got paid a fair wage, and it would be a lot better if more passengers appreciated their work. But until those two things happen, the most successful and happiest flight attendants will be embracing their art, not looking for someone to applaud them. If their airline started using hidden cameras and customer report forms to push them to do it more, they'd actually do it less. Manipulated art (even the art of service) ceases to be art.

World-class organizations hire motivated people, set high expectations, and give their people room to become remarkable.

THE INTERNET AS A GIFT SYSTEM

I often hesitate to use the phrase "gift economy," because as soon as I do, people wonder what they're going to get and how much they'll have to pay for it.

Clay Shirky and Doug Rushkoff have both talked about the public gift nature of the Internet. Someone puts a video up on YouTube, why? No obvious revenue potential, no ad sales, no clear path to fame. It's a gift.

At first, gifts can give life in a tiny realm. You do something for yourself, or for a friend or two. Soon, though, the circle of the gift gets bigger. The Internet gives you leverage. A hundred people read your blog or fifty subscribe to your podcast. There's no economy here, but there is an audience, a chance to share your gift.

And that circle begets other circles. The audience you charmed with your video realizes that they, too, can give a gift to the community. And so they do. And the audience continues to grow, each person enjoying the digital fruits of the labor that others donate to the ever-widening circle.

The fact that there's no organized cash or exchange system is part of what makes it work. If I send you two links and then you feel obligated to send me two links, we don't have art; we have an economy of reciprocity.

I didn't write my book to get anything from you in exchange. I wrote it because giving my small gift to the community in the form of writing makes me feel good. I enjoy that you enjoy it. When that gift comes back to me one day, in an unexpected way, I will enjoy the work I did twice as much.

Reciprocity defined as payment for my work isn't the point. It's the appreciation of my work, the way it changes businesses—that's my payment.

The Internet has taken the idea of gifts, multiplied it, and then pushed it into a realm where gifts previously haven't had much traction. The gift system is now a bigger part of commerce than it ever has been before. Margret Thatcher famously said, "There is no such thing as society." While this is ridiculous on the surface, the enlarging circle of gift culture demonstrates how false this statement is in practice. Society is where we give gifts.

Someone in our company publishes a paper about a new technique or gives a talk at a conference (for no pay). You go the extra mile to please a small customer or build an online forum to teach your customers how to get more out of your products (for no extra cost). These are all examples of the gift system at work. It works even more profoundly on an internal basis. Someone who is not in your department steps in and helps out during a crunch. A coworker shares his address book. You brainstorm a new idea with another salesperson. In each case, there's no reciprocity, no guarantee of repayment. Instead, there's an ever-enlarging circle, a circle where gifts are valued and passed on.

The only companies that don't benefit from this are the hoarders. Companies that take gifts but don't give them find themselves temporarily ahead of the game, but ultimately left out.

When your consumers appreciate your gift, they are saying, "Thank you and…"

Thank you and I told your boss what a wonderful thing you did.

Thank you and here's a record my band and I recorded last week.

Thank you and you made me cry.

Thank you and I just blogged about what you did.

Thank you and here's a twenty-dollar tip; I know it's not much, but it's all I can afford right now.

Thank you and how can I help you spread the word?

Thank you and can you teach me how to do that?

Thank you and you changed me, forever.

HOW TO ENCOURAGE GIFTS

Charging less money isn't the way to show respect to your consumers. Money is an essential element of making a living in this world, but money is a poor substitute for respect and thanks. Wall Street has learned this the hard way.

When someone patronizes your organization, order in lunch for him or her.

When someone delivers more than you asked for, give her more trust, more freedom, more leeway next time.

When someone gives a speech that exceeds the bar, don't merely circle "5" on the conference speaker review sheets. Instead, give him a standing ovation, wait to thank him after the talk, tell ten friends what you saw, and thank the conference organizer. It wasn't a transaction that you pay for with a few circles on a review sheet. It was a gift. If you want to repay it, do something difficult.

When a volunteer really steps up in your political campaign, don't just mumble a thank-you at the beginning of your next speech. Call her at home the next day and say thank you. Put her picture on your website. Insist on getting a photo shot with the two of you.

Respect is the gift you can offer in return.

11

❖ ❖ ❖

where is the GPS?

You must become indispensable to thrive in the new economy. The best ways to do that are becoming remarkable, insightful, an artist, a company bearing gifts. To lead. The worst way is to conform and become another bland company in a giant system.

WHAT DOES IT TAKE TO LEAD?

The key distinction is the ability to forge our own path, to discover a route from one place to another that hasn't been paved, measured, and quantified. So many times, we want someone to tell us exactly what to do, and so many times, that's exactly the wrong approach.

Growing up in Sierra Leone, the diamond cutters have an intrinsic understanding of the stone in their hands. They can touch and see exactly where the best lines are—they know. The greatest artists do just that. They see and understand the challenges before them, without carrying the baggage of expectations or attachment. The diamond cutter doesn't imagine the diamond he wants. Instead, he sees the diamond that is possible.

SEEING, DISCERNMENT, AND CHARITY

You can't make a map unless you can see the world as it is. You have to know where you are and where you're going before you can figure out how to go about getting there.

No one has a transparent view of the world. In fact, we all carry around a personal worldview—the biases and experiences and expectations that color the way we perceive the world.

The venture capitalist has a worldview shaped by his experience in funding dozens of companies over the years. He remembers the last bubble and the bubble before that, and he has the scars to prove it. So when you show him your business plan, he doesn't see only your plan. He also sees the echoes of past plans. He remembers other people, other days, and other ventures. And those memories color his perception.

The loyal employee has a worldview as well. She wants a stable place to work, and she believes in you. So when you show her your plan, her worldview changes her feelings and her analysis of your plan.

And the lawyer and the competitor and the skeptic and the mother-in-law each have their own worldviews, their own biases and expectations. None of us knows the absolute truth, of course, but the goal is to approach a situation with the least possible bias.

So the manager and the investor seek out companies with discernment, the ability to see things as they truly are. My mother might call this "charity." A life without attachment and stress can give you the freedom to see things as they are and call them as you see them. If you had this skill, what an asset you would be to any marketplace.

Of course, no one does this all the time. When we apply to college, we're attached to the outcome, so we're blinded by the reality of the process. When our company does layoffs, we're attached to the outcome, so we're blinded by the truth of the situation. Over and over, in the moments when we need to see our options the most clearly, we get stuck.

SEEING CLEARLY ISN'T EASY
It's difficult work, which is why it's so rare and valuable.

Seeing clearly means being able to look at a business plan from the point of view of the investor, the entrepreneur, and the market, but also the consumer. That's hard.

Seeing clearly means you're smart enough to know when a project is doomed, or brave enough to persevere when your competitors are fleeing for the hills.

Abandoning your worldview in order to try on someone else's is the first step in being able to see things as they are.

THE TWO REASONS SEEING THE FUTURE IS SO DIFFICULT
Attachment to an outcome combined with the resistance and fear of change.

That's it.

You have all the information that everyone else has. But if you are deliberately trying to create a future that feels safe, you will willfully ignore the future that is likely.

EFFORT CAN CHANGE THINGS

One of the fascinating aspects of business and organized movements is the correlation between the passion and effort that people bring to a project and its outcome.

This isn't true for the weather. Accept the day's forecast for what it is, because there's nothing you can do about it. But market share, innovation, negotiations, human relations—they can be shifted with the right sort of insight and effort.

The challenge is in understanding when our effort can't possible be enough, and in choosing projects and opportunities that are most likely to reward the passion we bring to a situation. If there's no way in the world you can please that customer with a reasonable amount of effort, perhaps it's better to accept the situation than it is to kill yourself trying (and failing) to change that person's mind-set.

There's a difference between passively accepting every element of your environment (and thus missing opportunities to exploit) and being wise enough to leave the unchangeable alone, or at least work around it.

SOMEONE ELSE, PLEASE BE IN CHARGE

My flight home was recently diverted to Richmond, Virginia. We were stuck at the gate, held hostage by the airline with a prognosis of a delay that would last somewhere from ninety minutes to five hours. Experienced travelers know that when the system breaks, it's broken. Bail!

I persuaded the flight attendant to give me permission to leave the plane. I had already gone online and found a rental car for $40. The drive to Washington, DC, was about ninety minutes. Clearly, this was a good bet.

I stood up to leave and said to the other twenty-three passengers, "I'm leaving and driving to Washington, DC. We'll be there in about two hours. If you want to join me, I have room for four other people, and it's free."

No one moved. I drove myself home.

I've thought about that a lot. Some of these people may have figured I was some sort of extremely well-dressed business traveler psychopath. My guess, though, is that most of them were very content to blame United for their situation. If they had stood up and left the plane, the situation would have belonged to them. Their choice, their responsibility.

SELF-DEFENSE

When you defend your position in the market, what are you defending?

Are you defending your past, your present, or the future you are nostalgic about?

The market doesn't care about your defense. It cares about working with someone who can accurately see what was, what is, and where things are headed. When you see a bump up ahead, do you say, "Oh my god, we're doomed!" Or do you say, "Isn't that interesting?"

When a vendor or a customer must choose between an organization working hard to defend the status quo and one that's open to big growth in the future, the choice is pretty simple.

There's no shortage of companies and no shortage of people willing to rearrange the truth to preserve their vision of the world, as they'd like it to be. There are lobbyists in Washington who make a great living helping corporations fight the inevitable future by arguing for protection. There are nonprofits that have long lost their reason to exist but are still maintained by management that doesn't have the guts to admit the world has passed them by. The same mind-set that drives people to stay in their home during a hurricane or massive blizzard is at work. Just because you want something to be true doesn't make it so.

Scarcity creates value, and what's scarce is a desire to accept what is and then work to change for the better, not deny that it exists.

THE AÇAI AND "CHARITY"

Worldview and attachment always color perceptions. Ask people in the customer service department about the biggest problem the company faces, and they will almost certainly define the challenge in terms of customer service. Ask the same question of those in finance, and of course, the answer will be based on the financial lens they use to see the world.

Açai Strong companies can't get attached to the object of their attention. The attachment to a worldview changes a company's relationship to what's happening and prevents them from converting what they see or interact with into something that belongs to them, something that they can work with and change.

A brilliant negotiator does her art by understanding the other side as honestly as anyone can. Only by seeing the world through clear eyes can she possibly craft a negotiation strategy that works for everyone.

It's very easy for us to become attached to our feelings and memories and expectations of the system we work in, the companies we invest in, and the people we work with. That attachment, and our response to it, forces us to wish for a different outcome from what we might honestly expect.

The executives in the record business, for example, loved their perfect business model. They were attached to their lifestyle and to the way their artist and fan relationships made them feel. When even a turnip could see that their business model was doomed, they soldiered on, apparently oblivious to the crumbling infrastructure around them. Were they stupid? No. They were blinded by their attachment to the present and their fear of the future.

Successful companies are able to see the threats of the past and the threads of the future and untangle them into something manageable.

The tangling is a natural state. Products, sunk costs, and complex systems conspire to weave the elements of our work into a matted mess. Things are the way they are, and it's difficult to perceive that they could be any other way.

The newspaper industry can't untangle news from paper, can't see the difference between delivering the news around the world for free and putting it on a truck for shipment down the block. As long as each of these elements is seen as inseparable from one another, it's impossible to untangle the future. That's why outsiders and insurgents so often invent the next big thing—they don't start with a tangled past.

The truth behind you and your customers' situation is no different. Your company may have a history with this customer; you may have a visceral memory of something that happened between your organization and the customer. Keep these ideas tangled, and there's no way you'll be flexible enough to partner with this customer for the future. You'll be too busy defending the past.

125

TELL THE TRUTH

First, of course, you have to be able to see the truth. This takes experience and expertise and, most of all, a willingness to look. But, wait, I have done that for you already.

Most people who see the truth refuse to acknowledge it. We can notice an unhappy customer, a crappy product, or a decaying industry, but we don't want to be aware of it. Our attachment is to a different future, so we ignore the data or diminish its importance. We don't mean to lie; we're in denial.

The few who can see the truth and become aware of it often hesitate to speak up. You don't want to upset the status quo. You fear the wrath of your competitors when they hear you say that the market is actually naked. You hesitate because you've been taught that this is not the work of a team player; it's the work of a rabble-rouser.

Smart organizations seek the ability to see the world as it actually is. But that skill is worthless if you don't acknowledge the truth and share it.

THE GUILT OF FRUSTRATED ARTISTS

The following is one of my favorite negative reviews of this book:

"Dumbuya doesn't explain how to go about doing the actual hard groundwork of leadership and art. He makes it sound like any company with an idea and a Twitter account can rally thousands of people to their cause in minutes if they just realize that it's not hard."

My response: Telling companies leadership is important is one thing. Showing them precisely how to be a leader is impossible. "Tell me what to do" is a nonsensical statement in this context.

There is no map—no map to be a leader, no map to be an artist. I've read hundreds of books about art (in all its forms) and how to do it, and not one has a clue about the map, because there isn't one.

Here's the truth that you have to wrestle with: the reason that art (writing, engaging, leading, all of it) is valuable is precisely why I can't tell you how to do it. If there were a map, there'd be no art, because art is the act of navigating without a map. No Siri, no GPS.

Don't you hate that? I love that there's no map.

12

❖ ❖ ❖

the choice is yours

Bill O'Neil is the most beloved banker in Lancaster County, Pennsylvania. He is the leading banker to the Amish community there, and he says he's never lost a single house to foreclosure.

Bill isn't Amish, but most of his customers are. He manages more than $100 million worth of loans for HomeTowne Heritage Bank, and at least $90 million of that is in mortgages for Amish farms.

O'Neil drives more than a thousand miles a week, visiting his customers and prospective borrowers. They have no credit history, none of the usual tools of his business. "I'll find out who his dad was," he says. "I'm also interested in who his wife's father was. It takes a team to make a farm go."

Part of the reason why his loan-and-hold approach is so successful is that he doesn't have much choice. He's legally forbidden from reselling the loans, because the houses have no electricity and no traditional homeowners insurance. As a result, if HomeTowne makes a loan, HomeTowne owns the loan.

That means, over the years, Bill has ended up on a first-name basis with almost all his customers. Here's a banker who's earning millions of dollars a year for his bank, doing business face-to-face, and making each connection more human, not less.

New business is easy to find. The Amish community remains tight-knit, and when a new farm is purchased, the family buying it can't help but hear all about Bill. It wouldn't take very much to undo all this positive word of mouth, and as a result, Bill holds himself even more accountable.

Bill doesn't own the bank. But he's indispensable. The asset Bill has built goes far beyond his book of business. Bill is açai—and his bank, a genius.

JOHN SELLS INSURANCE

I was standing at the bar of a boutique hotel, killing time, drinking club soda and gin, and chatting with the bartender before I went onstage to give a speech. It turns out that he was a full-time insurance salesman moonlighting as a bartender to make ends meet. He sold insurance to small businesses, door-to-door.

John was a veteran, recently back from Afghanistan. I was interested in his charisma and proud of his service, so we chatted. The amount of emotional labor he put into his work was obvious, and fascinated that people were still selling things door-to-door, I asked him about his day and his compensation. It turns out that 100 percent of his income was in commissions, and the company didn't really give him leads. Even worse, the company required him to use their business cards, their materials, and their script, at his expense. Not the perfect job, and certainly someone with John's interpersonal skills could do better. He was putting himself on the line, essentially acting as human spam, and getting paid a pittance to do it.

I started to give him some ideas on how he could gather better leads, how he could be more remarkable in his presentation, how he could turn a few casual customers into a larger group of truly committed customers.

Then John surprised me. He explained that he didn't want to risk anything that might work better, didn't want to leverage his time, didn't want to do anything except follow the rules. If he worked long enough and hard enough, he assured me, the system would pay off for him. He had gone from risking his life in the desert with IEDs to being afraid of a new way of selling insurance. The difference between John and your company is the taxes you file.

This upsets me. Of course John has a right to run his commission-based career any way he wants to. It's his choice. But John has been brainwashed, sold hard on not becoming açai. His company has given him a script, a set of rules, and has intimidated him into leaving his art at home. As a result, he ends up as a follower, a cog, and a quiet, reliable participant in the system.

Someone like John shouldn't have to moonlight to pay the bills.

THE CHOICE

You can either fit in or stand out. Not both.

You are either defending the status quo or challenging it: playing defense and trying to keep everything "all right" or leading and provoking and striving to make everything better.

Either you are embracing the drama of everyday business uncertainty or you are seeing the world as it is. These are all choices; you can't have it both ways.

Someone will support you because you fit the description, look right, have the right background, and don't ruffle feathers or because you are a dream come true, an agent of change sure to make a difference in both their lives and the products you are selling. I don't think it's possible to make this point too clearly. Being slightly remarkable is a losing strategy.

Indispensable and artistic companies work, and they are the future. But the in-between spaces are scary.

HEADS, YOU WIN

Perhaps the biggest shift the new economy brings is self-determination. Access to capital and appropriate connections aren't nearly as essential as they were. Remarkable companies are made, not born.

There's no doubt that environment still plays a huge role. The right timing or the right support or the right mentor are all still significant factors. But the new rules mean that even if you've got all the right background, you won't make it unless you choose to.

These are internal choices, not external factors. How we respond to the opportunities and challenges of the market now determines how much the outside world values us. In this section, I want to outline some of the roles the Açai Strong companies play and how you can choose to play them.

Will Opening More Hours Make You a Better Artist?

Does painting more pictures help? Writing more words? Inventing more inventions?

To a point.

But most of the time, that's not what açai companies do. Most of the time, we're doing nonaçai work,
doing someone else's work instead of our art. That's fine,
as long as there's a balance, as long as you leave enough
time for the work that matters.

The resistance encourages you to avoid the work,
and our markets reward busywork as well. Serious artists
distinguish between the work and the stuff they have to
do when they're not doing the work.

THE TYPICAL TRANSACTION

The typical transaction work look like this:
GIVE…GET…GIVE…GET…

The consumers give you a market for a product;
you do the work. In return, they give you money. It's an
exchange, one not so different from shopping at the local
store. The customer is the boss. He or she exchanges the
money for an item on the shelf, and both sides win.

Of course, if your store charges more than the competition, your customers will switch and buy from someone cheaper. As consumers, that's how they maximize
what they get for their money.

So what's missing?

The gift.

If you give your consumers the gift of art, insight,
initiative, or connection, they're less likely to shop around
every day looking to replace the commodity work you do,
because the work you do isn't a commodity.

LEARNING THE TOOLS

I'm always amazed when I meet a writer who can't
use a computer, or a lawyer who's uncomfortable with
LexisNexis, or an executive who needs a corporate IT

person to help him navigate an e-mail system. If you're a company that is unable to leverage your skills by using online tools, you're merely linked to the consumers.

The world just gave you control over the means of connection. Not to master them is a sin.

THE CHANGE

When big change hits, it is rarely gradual.

A hurricane hits, but the levee holds.

Then another one hits, and the levee holds.

There's no change from a normal day.

Then a big one hits, and the levee breaks.

One day, a system works; the next, it's underwater. The challenge here is that we can see the changes coming, and we try to deal with them by making incremental changes, by being timid, by waiting to see what happens. So by the time what is going to happen happens, we're toast.

In the circus, the only way to make it as a trapeze artist is to leap. And the company that brings change is able to do it just like that—leap.

When industries make transitions, 90 percent of the companies squander their momentum, waste their resources, and grudgingly tiptoe from the perfect market they were in and try to make their way over to the new opportunity. And along the way, those 90 percent are outfoxed, outgunned, and outwitted by the brave few.

With this new American Dream I'm talking about, this revolution in relevance, in mattering, in interacting, there isn't room for every company—not yet, anyway. Instead, we'll keep slots open until we have enough indispensable companies, until we have found the few businesses willing to abandon their overhyped products, throw out the rule book, and make a difference.

Then we'll get back to work.

DOES YOUR WORK MATCH YOUR PASSION? OR DOES YOUR PASSION MATCH YOUR WORK?

Conventional wisdom suggests that you should find work that matches your passion. I think this is backward.

I've argued repeatedly that your product should match your marketing, not the other way around, and the same inversion is true here. Transferring your passion to your market is far easier than finding a market that happens to match your passion.

FIT IN OR STAND OUT

There are countless MBAs waiting to tell you how to fit in, waiting to correct you, advise you, show you what you are doing wrong.

And no one pushes you to stand out.

If you add up all the books, scolds, backbenchers, bosses, teachers, parents, cops, coworkers, employees, religious zealots, politicians, and friends who can show you how to fit in just so, it's sort of overwhelming. It's clear to me that we're really good at establishing and reinforcing the status quo.

Fit in too much, though, and nothing much happens. Where are the self-appointed firebrands, the people who will egg you and push you to stand for something?

They seem to be missing.

HOW DOES BEING AN AÇAI COMPANY WORK?

In a world with only a few indispensable companies, the açai company has three elegant choices:

135

1. Hire plenty of factory workers. Scale like crazy. Take advantage of the fact that most companies want a map, most companies are willing to work cheaply, and most companies want to be the factory. You win because you extract the value of their labor, the labor they're surrendering to too cheaply.

2. Find a market that can't live without an açai company. Find consumers who adequately value your scarcity and your contribution, who will reward you with freedom and respect. Do the work. Make a difference.

3. Start your own gig. Understand that an organization that's açai is itself indispensable. Hire appropriately.

If you are not currently doing any of these initiatives, refuse to settle. You deserve better.

NOSTALGIA FOR THE FUTURE

For many companies, the happiest future is one that's precisely like the past, except a little better. We all enjoy nostalgia—the real kind, nostalgia for the past. We gladly suffer from that bittersweet feeling we get about successes we loved but can't relive. Nostalgia for the way we felt that first day we broke even or for that first year we passed our predictions.

We'd love to do it again, but we can't.

Nostalgia for the future is that very same feeling about things that haven't happened yet. We are prepared for them to happen, but if something comes along to change our future, those things won't happen, and we'll be disappointed.

If your company goes out of business, you may very well get another gig, but it won't be the job that, one day, was going to get you to the financial security you were imagining.

We're good at visualizing this future, and if we think it's not going to happen, we get nostalgic for it. This isn't positive visualization; it's attachment of the worst sort. We're attached to an outcome, often one we can't control.

Some businesspeople, though, have an itch for a different future, one with radically different rules. Those people are emotionally connected to the sort of drive and visionary leadership that organizations need. It's not a skill or even a talent. It's a choice. You don't want your head of business development to have serious nostalgia for a particular future. If she does, she'll hold on to the deals and structures that make that future appear, and undervalue alternatives that could dramatically improve your organization, at the same time that her future vision is threatened.

The *New York Times* was offered a deal with Amazon during the 1990s. It would have transformed the economics of the paper and delivered billions of dollars in revenue over time. According to former CEO Diane Baker, senior management turned it down. They were worried that they would upset Barnes & Noble, which at the time was a big advertiser. Management had nostalgia for a future with steady increases in their current business, and felt threatened by a radical shift in that future.

People with this affliction also run the book publishing business. They love their industry, their product, their systems, and the joy it brings them. New technologies and business systems undermine that vision, and publishers often dismiss them because of simple nostalgia. The same thing happened to Kodak and to the big accounting firms.

The açai company is able to invent a future, fall in love with it, live in it—and then abandon it on a moment's notice.

137

MADISON HOUSE AND PASSION

Madison House is a Colorado-based music management and booking firm. They represent artists like Bill Kreutzmann, The String Cheese Incident, and Los Lobos.

As the music world comes crashing down, they are thriving. How'd they do that?

Because of people like Nadia Prescher. Nadia is one of the people who runs the firm, and like her peers, she loves the music. She comes to the shows when she doesn't have to, works on details that aren't part of her job, and expends emotional labor because she can, not because she's told to.

Successful musicians have plenty of choices. If they pick Madison House, it's going to be because the people at the firm care enough to make a connection, not because they're the lowest-priced alternative. Every PR and professional service firm can learn from this. When your people do what they do because they love it, it works—even if they're not as technically adept as the competition.

BE THE AÇAI COMPANY ONCE

If your company can do it brilliantly once, just once, then of course you can do it again.

I'm not proposing you play a perfect round of golf or conduct a symphony. Instead, success lies in being generous or understanding someone or seeing a route that others don't see. You've done this already; do it brilliantly.

You've calmed yourself in the face of anxiety, or done something for no compensation, or solved a problem with an insight. Then, most of the time, the world steps in and relentlessly unteaches you how to do it again.

If you've done it once, you can do it again. Every day.

THIS IS WHAT HARD WORK LOOKS LIKE

No self-respecting salesperson complains about spending seven hours to fly to a prospect, give a twenty-minute pitch, and fly home.

No brave utility lineman complains about climbing a high-power tower to fix an insulator.

And no hardworking assembly-line worker hesitates about killing a hundred chickens an hour in the slaughterhouse.

That's because it's work. We're used to it, and we know how to do it.

Yet the work of inventing, brainstorming, and overcoming the fear of shipping appears too difficult to bear. The work of getting over an emotional reaction, seeing a situation as it really is, and caring enough to provide a gift—that's beyond the pale.

Nothing about becoming indispensable is easy. If it's easy, it's already been done, and it's no longer valuable.

What will make a company açai is not a shortcut. It's the understanding of which hard work is worth doing. The only thing that separates a great artist from a mediocre one is the ability to push through the resistance. Some companies decide that their art is important enough to overcome the resistance they face in doing their work. Those businesses become Açai Strong.

13

❖ ❖ ❖

connecting

If you can't sell your ideas, your ideas go nowhere. And if you flat-out lie about your ideas, we'll know and we'll reject them. The Internet amplifies both of these traits.

The new media rewards ideas that resonate. It helps them spread. If your work persuades, you prosper.

And the new media punishes those who seek to mislead. We have ever more refined truth-telling cues, meaning if you don't believe in what you're doing, we'll know, and you will fail. Honest signals are the only signals that travel—and they can do so without propulsion from you.

CREATING A CULTURE OF CONNECTION

Think about business-to-business sales. The key point of distinction between vendors calling on a company is rarely price. It's the perceived connection between the prospect and the organization.

Only a human being in an açai company can nurture these types of relationships. It has to be done with flair and transparency, and it can't be done from a script. The memories and connections and experiences of the company in the center of this culture are difficult to scale and hard to replace. Which makes this company indispensable.

RETURN ON CONNECTION INVESTMENT

Two people work in an investment bank. One has an MBA in finance, with a focus on using the Black-Scholes asset-pricing model to value options. He's a quant jock, and a pretty good one, at that. The other has pushed hard to become adept in working with people and, as a result, has personal relationships with twenty-seven of the bank's most important clients.

Guess which one is more valuable and more difficult to replace...

The Black-Scholes model is important, but it's easy to outsource or to do with a computer. Sure, a world-class quant jock is one in a million; that guy you want to hold on to. But a pretty good one? I'll take the human being over the computer every time.

THE SECRET OF RUBEN AT COMCAST

He's a real person.

That's the secret.

Ruben Eliason has been featured on the front page of the *New York Times*, on television, and online about a million times. Ruben is the online face of Comcast Cable, the occasionally loved, frequently hated cable behemoth.

Ruben figured out that angry customers were often using Twitter to vent their rage about Comcast and its service, or lack thereof.

One day, Ruben tweeted back.

He showed up. Not because it was in the manual or because someone told him to, but because he wanted to help. It was a gift, not his job. Ruben was honestly interested in connecting, and his generosity came through.

And you know what happened? The Twittersphere rejoiced. They were so stunned that a real person (with a name!) was listening that they instantly became fans. In less than a minute, they were converted from enemies and trolls into raving fans.

That's how desperately we want to be touched by another person. That's how much the gift of attention from a person means to us.

HE'S GOOD WITH PEOPLE

David works at ConEd in New York and has been recently promoted.

David's team visits neighborhoods that need new gas lines. His team digs up the street, shovels dirt, lays pipe, and keeps the system from falling apart. He's the young guy on the crew, but he makes more than most of the team.

That's because David is good with people. David is the guy who rings the doorbell, deals with angry neighbors, gets access to basements, and replaces shrubs— stuff that is essential, but is improvised.

ConEd can easily replace the flagman and the guy who runs the backhoe. Even the pipe fitters do a job that can be outsourced. David, on the other hand, is the key man, the Açai Strong employee.

Why is "being good with people" so diminished as a competency? Is it because we can't easily measure and quantify it? I think it's an art, which means that the person who provides it is an artist.

David can't write a play (at least not yet), but he's still an artist, and he benefits from his attitude every day. The attitude of the artist.

THE PROBLEM WITH THE SCRIPT

When companies give you a script to read, or when you use something from a how-to book, it almost never works. That's because you're not telling the truth, you're not being human, and you're not being transparent.

You might be parroting the words from the negotiation book or the public speaking training you went to, but all the smart people you encounter know that you're winging it or putting them on.

Virtually all of us make our living engaging directly with other people. When the interactions are genuine and transparent, they usually work. When they are artificial or manipulative, they fail.

The Açai Strong company is coming from a posture of generosity; it's there to give a gift. If that's your intent, the words almost don't matter. What we'll perceive are your wishes, not the script.

This is why telemarketing has such a ridiculously low conversion rate. Why corporate blogs are so lame. Why frontline workers in the service business have such stress. We can sense it when you read the script because we're so good at finding the honest signals.

GENUINE GIFTS

The only successful way to live in a world of honest signals is to give the genuine gift.

Genuine gifts, given with the right intent and a respectful posture, meet our sniff test. All our senses are on alert, and the giver passes the test. We believe.

Now that we believe, a different relationship can occur. One about "us," not just "you." But only if you cease to manipulate me and stop doing your job. Do your art instead. Change.

Let me restate this because it's so important.

We have everything we need, so we're not buying commodities. We're not even buying products. We're buying relationships and stories and magic. Our business, our politicians, and our friends—it's all the same; it's about figuring out whom we can trust and work with and who must be kept at bay.

Corporations tried to depersonalize all of those so they could lie to us, so they could package commodities, so they could scale without involving humans. And now they're out of steam. The corporatization is not working as well.

Since all you have to sell is relationships, you have to bypass the scam filters. You can certainly try to be the rational best-price, most-convenient alternative. But if you can't do that (and who can?), then the only path available to you is to change me, connect with me, or make a difference in my life.

Walmart wins because it's cheap and close. Everyone else who wins must do so by being generous.

And for that, you must be an artist, and you need to mean it.

THE PLACEBO EFFECT

It's been demonstrated again and again that the placebo effect makes people get better. When a trusted doctor gives you medicine, odds are it will make you feel better (it may even cause you to get better), even if the medicine is only a sugar pill.

Honest signals are the explanation.

If the doctor truly believes, truly cares, and can see us for who we are, we can sense that. It doesn't matter what she says; it matters what else we pick up in our interactions with her. The words don't cure us; our beliefs do.

If the placebo effect is enough to cure cancer (and it can), then it can change your client's mind and dramatically shift the way people perceive your organization. The same autosuggestion that heals bodies also changes minds. The people you deal with make instant, and often permanent, decisions about people, products, and organizations. Humans are not rational computing machines—far from it.

The people you work with won't change if you don't believe. The communication of enthusiasm and connection and leadership in your market starts with the gift you give, not with the manipulation you attempt.

14

❖ ❖ ❖

seven açai strong traits

Açai companies do two things for the market: they exert emotional labor, and they make a map. Those contributions take many forms. Here is one way to think about the list of what makes you indispensable:

1. Providing a unique interface between members of the organization

2. Delivering unique creativity

3. Managing a situation or organization of great complexity

4. Leading customers

5. Inspiring staff

6. Providing deep domain knowledge

7. Possessing a unique talent

A UNIQUE INTERFACE BETWEEN MEMBERS OF THE ORGANIZATION

If your organization is a network (and it is), what holds that network together?

Is it just the salary and each person's fear of losing his or her job? If so, you've already lost.

In a story so good that it should be apocryphal, Zappos offers graduates of their two-week paid training $2,000 if they will quit their new jobs. Why would Zappos offer to pay great people to quit? Tony Hsieh, CEO, does this because he wants to make sure that every person at the company is there for the right reasons, not because he or she is getting paid. If you're willing to leave for a few thousand bucks, good riddance.

In great organizations, there's a sense of mission. The company is racking up accomplishments, going somewhere. That mission doesn't happen accidentally. An açai employee helps lead, and he or she connects people in the organization, actively and with finesse. This takes emotional labor, and it can't be done by following the instructions in a manual.

The organization also includes its customers and prospects. That means if you are the person who provides the bridge between the outside world and the company, you are in a critical position.

In most organizations, people do these jobs because they have to, and they do them to spec. But occasionally, you find someone who relishes the opportunity. Darienne Page is the first civilian you meet if you're called to a meeting with Barack Obama at the White House. As the official receptionist of the United States, she views her job as an opportunity to make a connection.

In the moments between you being checked through security and arriving at her tiny office, she'll have Googled you. She'll be ready with not just a warm welcome and a smile, but with relevant information you can chat about. She's looking forward to the engagement; it's her chance to perform, to do some art.

Certainly, the White House would function without Darienne Page. But by escalating the job above the manual, she changes it.

DELIVERING UNIQUE CREATIVITY

Three fairly simple words, but very difficult to combine in a meaningful way. Let's go backward: creativity is personal, original, unexpected, and useful.

Unique creativity requires domain knowledge, a position of trust, and the generosity to actually contribute. If you want to create a unique guitar riff, it sure helps if you've heard all the other guitar riffs on record. Unique implies that the creativity is focused and insightful.

Delivering unique creativity is hardest of all, because not only do you have to have insight, but you also need to be passionate enough to risk the rejection that delivering a solution can bring. You must ship.

The resistance, our fear of standing out, rears its ugly head every time we're on the hook for this sort of work. So we avoid the work. The sparse list of companies willing (and able) to do this sort of work makes it particularly valuable.

MANAGING A SITUATION OR ORGANIZA-TION OF GREAT COMPLEXITY

When the situation gets too complex, it's impossible to follow the manual, because there is no manual. That's why açai employees are so valuable during times of great complexity (which is most of the time). These employees make their own maps and thus allow the organization to navigate more quickly than it ever could if it had to wait for the paralyzed crowd to figure out what to do.

When I helped run a summer camp in Falls Church, Virginia, at the Center For Multicultural Human Services, the craziest day of the year was travel day, with dozens of kids going to dozens of places around the state, all at the same time.

We had buses and cars to coordinate. Parents on the phone, parents at the bus terminals, and parents who forgot to show up.

Out of twenty staff members, only a dozen could be trusted to handle travel day. They were ambassadors, cut off from the king, making decisions on their own in a foreign land. The good ones were priceless.

All of our staff members were great, but most couldn't handle this task. It required mapmaking and clear judgment, and if you hadn't practiced either, it was hard to invent on the fly. This isn't a gift you're born with; it's a choice.

LEADING CUSTOMERS

As market fragments and audiences spread, consumers are seeking connections more than ever. In short, we're looking for companies to follow and for others to join us as we do.

In the traditional model of commerce, a tiny group defines a product or a brand, and teams of people go sell it. It's a one-way transaction and it's static. Tide detergent is Tide detergent; take it or leave it.

The new model is interactive, fluid, and decentralized. That means organizations need more than a tiny team. It means every person who interacts with a consumer—or a business being sold to, or a donor to a nonprofit, or a voter—is doing marketing as leadership.

There's no script for leadership. There can't be.

INSPIRING STUFF

Organizations obey Newton's laws. A team at rest tends to stay at rest. Forward motions aren't the default state of any group of people, particularly groups with lots of people.

In a factory, this isn't really a problem. The owner controls the boss who controls the foreman who controls the worker. It's a tightly linked chain, and things get done because there is cash to be made. Most modern organizations are now far more amorphous than this. Responsibility isn't as clear, deliverables aren't as measurable, and goals aren't as cut-and-dried. So things slow down.

The açai employee changes that. Understanding that your job is to make something happen changes what you do all day. If you can only cajole, not force, if you can only lead, not push, then you make different choices.

You can't say, "Get more excited and insightful, or you're fired." Actually, you can, but it won't work. The front desk worker at a hotel who runs out in the middle of the night to buy gym shorts for a guest isn't doing it out of fear of being reprimanded. He does it because he was inspired to do so by a leader who wasn't even in the hotel when the clerk decided to contribute.

PROVIDING DEEP DOMAIN KNOWLEDGE

Earlier, I argued that having deep domain knowledge by itself is rarely sufficient to becoming indispensable. Combining that knowledge with smart decisions and generous contributions, though, changes things. Lester Wunderman knows quite a bit about direct marketing.

In fact, he invented it. He helped create the American Express card and the Columbia Record Club.

In watching Lester, it turns out that we didn't learn a thing about the tactics of direct marketing from him. Instead, my team learned about decision making and strategy. We came to understand the big personalities in the industry as well as the motivations of many of our partners. Mentoring is rarely about the face of the deal (the faces are easily found) but, instead, is a transfer of emotion and confidence. Lester had drawn a map once before, so he had the standing and authority to help us draw a new map.

Mapmakers often have the confidence to draw maps because they understand their subject so deeply.

POSSESSING A UNIQUE TALENT

When I was a kid, I loved the *Legion of Super-Heroes* and the *Justice League of America*. These were comics for slumming comic book writers, fun and sort of stupid stories in which a whole bunch of superheroes would get together, hang out in the clubhouse, and then work as a team to destroy some sort of monster that any individual superhero never could have bested.

Anyway, near the beginning of most of these comics was a scene where a stranger would meet the team. Inevitably, the superheroes would introduce themselves. Of course, Batman and Superman wouldn't need an introduction, but the lesser (lower-rent) heroes had to speak up and describe their superpowers.

"I'm the Wasp. I have the ability to shrink to a height of several centimeters, fly by means of insecticide wings, and fire energy blasts."

Some fancy marketers might call this a positioning statement or a unique selling proposition. Of course, it's not that. It's a superpower.

When someone meets your company, you need to have a superpower. If you don't, you're just another handshake. It's not about touting yourself or coming on too strong. It's about making the introduction meaningful. If I don't know your superpower, then I don't know how you can help me—or how I can help you.

When I tell the superpower story to people, they seem to get it. But then you look at their superpower, and it's something that might be a power, but it isn't really super. It's sort of an average power. "Pleasant and compliant" is the one we've been taught. Sorry, that's good, but it's not super.

If you want to be açai, the power you bring to the table has to be very difficult to replace. Be bolder and think bigger. Nothing is stopping you.

It's possible that no one ever pushed you to be brave enough to go this far out on a limb. Consider yourself pushed.

COMPLIANCE AND HUMILITY

At some level, all companies are virtuous, powerful, and wise. But none of these gifts works all the time. We'll stray from our principles, falter in our efforts, or make a bad decision now and then. Which is why humility is so important.

Humility is our antidote to what's inevitably not going to go according to plan. Humility permits us to approach a problem with kindness, not arrogance.

But humility is not the same as compliance. Humility doesn't mean meekness or fitting in at all costs.

153

Compliance feels like a shortcut to humility because it permits us to deny responsibility for whatever goes wrong. But compliance deprives you of your superpower; it robs you of the chance to make something better.

The challenge, then, is to be the generous artist, but do it knowing that it just might not work. And that's okay.

15

❖ ❖ ❖

when it doesn't work (well)

What happens when the conversation doesn't happen, the product doesn't sell, the consumer is not delighted, and the people aren't moved?

Make more art.

It's the only choice, isn't it?

GIVE MORE GIFTS

Learn from what you did and then do more.

The only alternative is to give up and to become an outdated business model. Which means failing. Trying and failing is better than merely failing, because trying makes you an artist and gives you the right to try again.

MAYBE YOU CAN'T GET PAID FOR DOING YOUR ART

The thing is, it's far easier than ever before to surface your ideas, far easier to have someone notice your interpersonal skills or your writing or your vision. Which means that companies that might have hidden their talents are now finding them noticed.

That blog you've built, the one with a lot of traffic—perhaps it can't be monetized.

That nonprofit you work with, the one where you are able to change lives—perhaps turning it into a career will ruin it.

That passion you have for abstract painting—perhaps making your work commercial enough to sell will squeeze the joy out of it.

When what you do is what you love, you're able to invest more effort and care and time. That means you're more likely to win, to gain share, to profit. On the other hand, poets don't get paid. Even worse, poets who try to get paid end up writing jingles and failing and hating it at the same time.

Today, there are more ways than ever to share your talents and hobbies in public. And if you're driven, talented, and focused, you may discover that the market loves what you do—that people read your blog or click on your cartoons or listen to your MP3s. But, alas, that doesn't mean you can monetize it, quit your day job, and spend all day writing songs.

The pitfalls:

1. In order to monetize your work, you'll probably corrupt it, taking out the magic, in search of dollars.

AND

2. Attention doesn't always equal significant cash flow.

156

I think it makes sense to make your art your art, to give yourself over to it without regard for commerce. (It will sell itself.)

Doing what you love is as important as ever, but if you're going to make a living at it, it helps to find a niche where money flows as a regular consequence of the success of your idea. Loving what you do is almost as important as doing what you love, especially if you need to make a living at it. Go do the job you can commit to, a career or a business you can fall in love with.

A friend who loved music, who wanted to spend his life doing it, got a job doing PR for a record label. He hated doing PR and eventually realized that simply being in the record business didn't mean he had anything at all to do with the music. Instead of finding a job he could love, he ended up being in proximity to, but nowhere involved with, something he cared about. I wish he had become a committed schoolteacher instead, spending every minute of his spare time making music and sharing it online for free. Instead, he's a frazzled publicity house, working twice as many hours for less money and doing no music at all.

Maybe you can't make money doing what you love (at least what you love right now). But I bet you can figure out how to love what you do to make money (if you choose wisely).

Do your art. But don't wreck your art if it doesn't lend itself to bringing in revenue. That would be a tragedy.

(And the twist, because there is always a twist, is that as soon as you focus on your art and leave the money behind, you may discover that this focus turns out to be the secret of actually breaking through and making money.)

157

THE ENDLESS GIVING CYCLE OF ART

When companies are committed to their art, what you'll discover is this: they never stop giving.

They don't give for a while, hoping to get, and then, once they cross a threshold, become takers. Instead, they have a posture of always giving. That's what they do, because they are artists, not cogs. They are Açai Strong, not replaceable employees.

What you're doing might not be working, and you might not be able to do what you're doing and get paid for it. But I am certain that if you give enough, to the right people, in the right way, your gifts will be treasured, and your journey will be rewarded. Even if that's not why you're doing it.

16

❖ ❖ ❖

in perspective

I didn't set out to get you to stop offering your products or services.

All I wanted to do in this book was sell you on being the artist and entrepreneur you already are. To make a difference. To stand for something. To get the respect and security you deserve in your market.

If I've succeeded, then you know that you have a gift to give, something you can do to change the world— or your part of it—for the better. I hope you'll do that, because we need you.

WHAT WILL YOU CHOOSE?

This is the scary part, of course. Your bluff is called. The barrier to success going forward isn't being cheap or reliving your golden days.

There's no indication that you need to be a company with a set of gifts or a world-class talent, either.

It's so easy to try to compromise, to do both, to fit in AND stand out. Try for both, you may say. Therein lies failure. There's no room for compromise here, because those who are competing with you are specializing. They're going to obsess about either fitting in or standing out. THE ACT OF DECIDING IS THE ACT OF SUCCEEDING.

The barrier to success is a choice. Up to you.

NO REGRETS

There's a popular brand of clothing with a huge slogan plastered on it: NO FEAR.

I think this motto is either disingenuous or stupid. Of course you should have fear. Riding a bike without a helmet may be fearless, but it's not smart. Lava surfing may be fearless as well, but we can all agree it's not smart, either.

So, what's smart? Creating a company without regret. Now that you know what to call the fear that has held you back all these years, what are you going to choose to do about the resistance? Now that you understand that society rewards you for standing out, for giving gifts, for making connections and being remarkable, what are you going to choose to do with that information?

You have a genius inside of you, a "charity" with something to share with the world. Everyone does. Are you going to continue hiding it, holding it back, and settling for less than you deserve just because you are afraid?

Therein lies regret.

CAN YOU CHANGE EVERYTHING?

You might not be as permanently stuck in a rut as you think. The rut you're in isn't permanent, nor is it perfect. There are certainly less perfect ruts, and there may be better ones as well. The certain thing is that you can change everything—if you choose to.

Critics have been brainwashing you into settling for a long time. It's easy to view your current situation as a box, a set of boundaries from which there is no escape. Of course you need to keep living your life the way you've been living it, because to do anything but that is too scary, too risky, too bold.

And yet…

And yet, every day, a few companies (more than a few companies) change everything. You can do it. You can embrace a new path and take it. Don't settle. You're a genius, and we need your contribution.

Do the work. Please.

LAST WORD

We can't profitably get more average.

We can't get more homogenized, more obedient, or cheaper. We can't get faster, either.

We've gone against our true nature and corporatized, anonymized, and dehumanized as many of our systems as we possibly can. Even health care is a system now, not a human interaction. We could probably go even further, actually, but I'm betting it won't be a fun or profitable journey.

If all mortgages are the same, of course they can be chopped up and remixed and resold. But that means all bankers and all homes are the same, and so are all homeowners. Which means the cheap ones or the profitable ones are all that matter. If all online products at all online stores are the same, then of course I'll use a price-shopping website to find the cheapest product.

If all employees are nothing but a résumé, and résumés can be scanned, then why are we surprised that our computers end up finding us anonymous average people to fill our anonymous average jobs?

If every restaurant on the highway will give me precisely the same cheery service from the same robotic staff, at the same prices, then why does it matter where I stop?

DO WE NEED TO BE FLATTER AND SMALLER?

It's our desire to be treated like individuals that will end this system. Our passion for contribution and possibility, the passion we've drowned out in school and in the corporate world—that's the only way out.

Every successful organization is built around people. Humans who do art. People who interact with other people. Men and women who don't merely shuffle money, but interact, give gifts, and connect.

All these interactions are art. Art isn't only a painting; it's anything that changes someone for the better, an anonymous interaction that leads to a human (not simply a commercial) conclusion.

Art can't be bought and sold. It must contain an element that's a gift, something that brings the artist closer to the viewer, not something that insulates one from the other. So we need to remember how to be artists.

Artists, at least the great ones, see the world more clearly than the rest of us. They have "charity," a sense of what actually is, not simply the artists' take on it. That honest sight allows the artist to see the future over the cloudy horizon. As our world changes faster and faster, it is these honest artists who will describe our future and lead us there.

The only thing keeping you from being one of these artists is the resistance. The loud voice of fear telling you that you can't possibly do it, that you don't deserve it, that people will laugh at you. We don't have a talent shortage; we have a shipping shortage. Anyone who makes the choice to overcome the resistance and has the insight to make the right map can become Açai Strong.

You can't fake it, though, because human beings are too talented at sensing when a gift is not a gift, when we're being played or manipulated. And sometimes, our art isn't enough. It's not enough to get us a sale or even a living. But we persist because making art is what we do.

The result of this art, these risks, the gifts, and the humanity coming together is both wonderful and ironic. The result of getting back in touch with our precommercial selves will actually create a post-commercial world that feeds us, enriches us, and gives us the stability we've been seeking for so long.

Be brave.

Be daring.

Be AÇAI STRONG.

antioxidants

DELIVERING UNIQUE CREATIVITY

- Is JetBlue Airways juicing? Their low-cost structure, underused airports, and young, nonunion staff gives them an unfair advantage.

- Is Starbucks juicing? They invented the coffee bar phenomenon, and now whenever we think coffee, we think Starbucks.

- Is Vanguard juicing? Their low-cost index funds make it impossible for a full-service broker to compete.

- Is Amazon.com juicing? Their free shipping and huge selection give them an unfair advantage over the neighborhood store.

- Is Google juicing? They learned from the mistakes of the first-generation portals, and they don't carry the baggage of their peers.

- Is Wendy's juicing? Their flexibility allows them to introduce half a dozen salad-based entrées, capturing a big chunk of the adult market.

- Is Ducati juicing? Because they don't have to make motorcycles for the entire market, they can specialize in amazing high-profit bikes, which sell out every year.

None of these companies are using performance-enhancing business supplements or old-fashioned techniques to win. To their entrenched (but nervous) competitors, these companies appear to be "juicing" because they're not playing by the rules.

Why aren't you juicing?

CHIP CONLEY

Chip Conley runs more than a dozen hotels in San Francisco. His first hotel, the Phoenix, is in one of the worst neighborhoods downtown. Chip got the hotel—a motel, really—for next to nothing. He knew that it wasn't a hotel for everybody. In fact, no matter what he did to the Phoenix, hardly anyone would choose to stay there.

Which is fine. Because "hardly anyone" can be quite enough if you've got a hotel with just a few dozen rooms. Chip redesigned the place. He painted it funky colors. Put hip style magazines in all the rooms. Had a cutting-edge artist paint the inside of the pool. And invited up-and-coming rock-and-roll stars to stay at the place.

Within months, the plan worked. By intentionally ignoring the mass market, Chip created something remarkable: a rock-and-roll motel in the center of San Francisco. People looking for it found it.

If that is considered juicing, I'll take a shot of açai.

LEADING CUSTOMERS AND THE MARKET

Why do birds fly in formation? Because the birds that follow the leader have an easier flight. The leader breaks the wind resistance, and the following birds fly far more efficiently. Without the triangle formation,

Canadian Geese would never have enough energy to make it to the end of their long migration.

A lot of risk-adverse businesspeople and businesses believe that they can follow a similar strategy. They think they can wait until a leader demonstrates a breakthrough idea, and then rush to copy it, enjoying the break in wind resistance from the leader.

If you watch closely, though, you'll notice that the flock alternates its formation. Every few minutes, one of the birds from the back of the flock will break away, fly to the front, and take over, giving the previous leader a chance to move to the back and take a break.

The problem with companies that avoid a remarkable market opportunities is they never end up as the leader. They are doing what they are told, staying within the boundaries, and following instructions. Alas, they usually pick the wrong lead bird.

Even if you find a flock that's pretty safe, in our turbulent world, it's harder and harder to stay in formation, and we often find ourselves scurrying to find a new flock. The ability to lead is thus even more important, because when your flock fades away, there may be no other flock handy.

PROVIDING DEEP DOMAIN KNOWLEDGE

Lionel Poilane's dad was a French baker, and he inherited the family bakery when he was a young man. Rather than sitting still and tending to the fires, though, Lionel became obsessed with being remarkable.

He did extensive research, interviewing more than eight thousand French bakers about their technique. He pioneered the use of organic flour in France. He refused to bake baguettes, pointing out that they were fairly tasteless and very un-French, as they were a fairly recent import from Vienna. He acquired the largest collection of bread cookbooks in the world—and studied them.

His sourdough bread is made with just flour, water, starter, and sea salt, and it's baked in a wood-fire oven. Poilane refused to hire bakers—he told me they had too many bad habits to unlearn—and instead hired young men who were willing to apprentice with him for years.

At first, the French establishment rejected his products, considering them too daring and different. But the overwhelming quality of the loaves and Poilane's desire to do it right finally won them over.

Virtually every fancy restaurant in Paris now serves Poilane bread. People come from all over the world to wait in line in front of his tiny shop on Rue de Cherche Midi to buy a huge loaf of sourdough bread—or more likely, several loaves. The company he founded now ships loaves all over the world, turning handmade bread into a global product, one worth talking about.

Lionel has sold more than $20 million worth of bread.

açai strong chews

- It's not an accident that some products catch on and some don't. When word of mouth occurs, it's often because all the viral pieces work together. How smooth and easy is it to spread your idea? How often will people tell it to their friends? How tightly knit is the group you're targeting? Do they talk much? Do they believe each other? How reputable are the people most likely to promote your idea? How persistent is it? Is it an idea that has to spread fast before it dies? Or will the idea have legs and thus you can invest in spreading it over time?

Put all your new product developments through this analysis, and you'll discover which ones are most likely to catch on. Those are the products and ideas worth launching. They catch on because of the art in them.

- Differentiate your customers. Find the group that's most profitable. Find the group that's most likely to promote your ideas. Figure out how to develop/advertise/reward either group. Ignore the rest. Your products shouldn't cater to the masses. Your products should cater to the customers you'd choose if you could choose your customers.

- What tactics does your firm use that involve following the leader? What if you abandoned them and did something very different instead? Art. If you acknowledge that you'll never catch up by being the same, make a list of ways you can catch up by being different.

- Do you have the e-mail addresses of the 20 percent of your customer base that loves what you do? If not, start getting them. If you do, what would you make for these customers that would be super-special?

- What would happen if you took one or two seasons off from the new-product grind and reintroduced wonderful classics instead? What sort of amazing things could you offer in the first season you came back (with rested designers)?

- Go to a science fiction convention. These are pretty odd folks. Do you appeal to an audience as wacky and wonderful as this one? How could you create one? (Jeep did. So did Fast Company and the Longaberger Basket Company. There are similar groups in the investing community, the market for operating systems, and the market for million-dollar stereo systems. Products differ, but most consumers and early adopters stay the same.)

- Where does your product end and marketing hype begin? The Dutch Boy Can is clearly product, not hype. Can you redefine what you sell in a similar way?

- If you're in an intangibles business, your business card and website is a big part of what you sell. What if everyone in your company had to carry a second business card? Something that actually sold them (and you). Something remarkable. Now, go do it!

- If someone in your organization is charged with creating an Açai Strong product, leave them alone! Don't use internal reviews and usability testing to figure out if the new product is as good as what you've got now. Instead, pick the right maverick and get out of the way.

- Go take a design course. Send your designers to a marketing course. And both of you should spend a week creating art.

- Is there someone (a person, an agency?) in your industry who has a track record of successfully launching remarkable products? Can you hire them away, or at least learn from their behavior? Immerse yourself in fan magazines, trade shows, design reviews—whatever it takes to feel what your fans feel.

- Can you create a culture of aggressively prototyping new products and policies? When GM shows a concept car at the New York Auto Show, there's more than ego involved. They're trying to figure out what car nuts think is remarkable. I'm not pitching focus groups here—they're a waste. I'm talking about the very public release of cheap prototypes, to get insight.

- Remarkable isn't always about changing the biggest machine in your factory. It can be the way you answer your phone, launch a new brand, or price a revision to your software. Getting in the habit of doing the "unsafe" thing every time you have the opportunity is the best way to learn to project—you get practice at seeing what's working and what's not.

- If you could build a competitor that had costs that were 30 percent lower than yours, could you do it? If you could, why don't you?

- References available upon request? Nonsense. Your references are your résumé. A standard résumé is nothing but an opportunity for a prospective employer to turn you down. A sheaf of over-the-top references, on the other hand, begs for a meeting.

- Visit www.monster.com, with millions of résumés, all in a pile, all waiting for someone to find them. If you're in that pile, it's not a good place to be. Consider what you could do today so you never have to worry about that.

- The big question is this: Do you want to grow? If you do, you need to embrace the Açai Strong mantra. You can maintain your brand the old way, but the only route to healthy growth is a remarkable product and art.

WHAT DO I DO NOW?

acknowledgments

Neil Irwin, Indigo Johnson, Scott Finklestein, Todd Garland, Sheryl Sandberg, Vicky Thompson, Irv Shapiro, Earnest Baylor, Shirley Baylor, Daphne Dean, The Professor, Georgia Bennett, Solomon Agyei, Shanna Akanbi, Michael Dadashi, Lee Chen, Gordon Jones, Tony DiConstanzo, Malcolm Robinson, Will Gruver, Demetra Baylor, Zoë Amenah Dumbuya, Alusine Conteh, Wusu Sesay, Eric Perry, Lester Johnson, Gregory Bolden, Matt o'Hayer, Brian Lash, Suzanne Evans, Jack Wilson, Dr. Tenielle Walker, Larry Borden, Charles Feit, E. Seignious, Armando Montelongo, Kevin Lowe, Sean Jensen, Tony Jimenez, Pramod Bonavar, Bo Clift, Mark Eldridge, Bobby Harris, Horace Campbell, Heidy Sweeney, Al Espinosa, Corey Rogers, Dries Buytaert, the entire staff at Global Publishing & Media Group, and the wonderful folks at the Marketing Republik. Special thanks to the people who read the acknowledgments. You know who you are.

And, of course, my mom and dad, for pushing me to be an artist long before knowing what it meant.

reading list

Here is a list of some of the amazing books I had the pleasure of reading while working on *Açai Strong*. To the authors: Thank you. You gave me seeds that I nursed into generous crops—crops that I hope will nourish businesses and entrepreneurs.

On Gifts and Art:

- *The War of Art*, by Steven Pressfield
- *Linchpin: Are you indispensable?* by Seth Godin
- *The Gift*, by Lewis Hyde
- *Art is Work*, by Milton Glaser
- *Man on Wire*, by Philippe Petit
- *True and False*, by David Mamet

On Sociology and Economics:

- *The Lonely Crowd*, by David Riesman, with Nathan Glazer and Reuel Denney
- *From the American System to Mass Production: 1800–1932*, by David Hounshell
- *The Power Elite*, by C. Wright Mills
- *The American Myth of Success: From Horatio Alger to Norman Vincent Peale*, by Richard Weiss

- *The Managed Heart: Commercialization of Human Feeling*, by Arlie Russer Hochschild
- *Stone Age Economics*, by Marshall Sahlins
- *Life Inc.: How the World Became a Corporation and How to Take it Back*, by Douglas Rushkoff
- *The Protestant Ethic and Spirit of Capitalism*, by Max Weber
- *The Communist Manifesto*, by Karl Marx and Friedrich Engels
- *The Wealth of Nations*, by Adam Smith
- *The Big Sort: Why the Clustering of Like-minded America is Tearing us Apart*, by Bill Bishop
- *The Rise of the Creative Class: And How it's Transforming Work, Leisure, Community and Everyday Life*, By Richard Florida
- *The Trap: Selling out to Stay Afloat in Winner-take-all America*, By Daniel Book

On Education:

- *Weapons of Mass Instruction*, by John Taylor Gafto
- *Schooling Capitalist America*, by Samuel Bowles and Herbert Gintis
- *Learning to Labor: How Working-class Kids Get Working-class Jobs*, by Paul Willis

On Programming and Productivity:

- *The Mythical Man-Month: Essays on Software Engineering*, by Frederick P. Brooks, Jr.

- *Joel on Software*, by Joel Spolsky
- *Zen Habits*, by Leo Babauta

On Science, the Brain, and Evolution:

- *Ever Since Darwin: Reflections in Natural History*, by Stephen Jay Gould
- *Iconoclast: A Neuroscientist Reveals how to Think Differently*, by Gregory Berns
- *How We Decide*, by Jonah Lehrer

On Wisdom:

- *Ignore Everybody: And 39 Other Keys to Creativity*, by Hugh McLeod
- *The Black Swan: The Impact of the Highly Improbable*, by Nassim Nicholas Taleb

On Getting Creative:

- *Getting Things Done: The Art of Stress Free Productivity*, by David Allen
- *Presentation Zen: Simple Ideas on Presentation Design and Delivery*, by Garr Reynolds

about the author

Wusu Dumbuya Jr. is the author of several upcoming books, including *Disposable Marketing* and *Our Time to Lead*. His blogs and perspective in marketing and management have changed the way businesspeople think and act. He is founder and CEO of the Marketing Republik, a boutique and highly selective international marketing firm. He lives in the Washington, DC, metropolitan area. Follow him on Twitter (@wdumbuyajr) to get familiar.

e-mail: contact@wusudumbuyajr.com
website: wusudumbuyajr.com